"ABIDE IN THE VINE"
Living At Face Level
With Jesus Christ!

BY

CHUCK LAMKA

ISBN 978-0-9846849-1-5
Copyright:
Little Light Ministries Unlimited 2011
Published by His Vineyard Productions
His Vineyard has been the voice of Little Light Ministries
Unlimited since 1977.
10611 Canyon Road East PMB 230
Puyallup, WA 98373

As I wrote this book there were many memories that filled my mind and contributed to the examples that appear in the book. This book is personally dedicated to my two extreme athlete sons, Peter and Joshua, who mean everything in the world to me and is also dedicated to all those who choose to commit their lives to Jesus Christ and strive daily to Abide in the Vine!

May your life be filled with excitement, contentment and the love, joy and peace of the Lord as you travel the river of life, abiding in Christ and living at Face Level with Him.

In the Service of Our Lord and Saviour,

Chuck Lamka

Forward

As you delve into the following pages it may not read like a novel for the purpose is not to entertain nor is it simply to educate but instead it is meant to draw each of us into a deep abiding relationship with the Lord where we become like Him and bear much fruit for the Kingdom of God.

In the fourteen chapters that follow each is designed to display our weaknesses and help us to overcome them as we grow and are daily being made into the likeness of Christ. It is also designed to show us that the abiding life is an intimate relationship that only brings forth life as we remain faithful with our eyes firmly fixed on the one who gave all to be able to present us blameless unto the Father without spot or blemish having become victorious in all things.

Each and every chapter is in its self an important lesson to be learned as we abide in the vine living and Walking in the Spirit and growing in grace with the Word of God abiding within.

It is the hope of the author that as you read that you will discover the beautiful Tapestry of the portrait of Christ that is the Bible and that you will come to understand and love the Word of God for Christ is the Word and every word written in the Bible either describes something about Him or His creation or His relationship with you and I who are His creation.

ABIDE IN THE VINE

Chapter One--- "Beginning the Tapestry" 'Entering the White water'

Chapter Two---- "Believe, Trust and Abide"

Chapter Three---- "Baptized"

Chapter Four---- "Tossed To and Fro"

Chapter Five---- "Faith"

Chapter Six---- "The Living Word"

Chapter Seven---- "Fully Equipped"

Chapter Eight---- "No Turning Back"

Chapter Nine---- "Facing your Fears"

Chapter Ten----- "A True Disciple and Yielded Servant" 'The Way Up is Down'

Chapter Eleven---- "The Missed Gate"

Chapter Twelve---- "A 'Rapid' Change"

Chapter Thirteen---- "A Victorious Finish"

Chapter Fourteen---- "Beyond The Finish Line"

Chapter I

"Beginning The Tapestry"

'Entering The White Water'

Of all the great truths found in the Word of God setting forth the abiding life in Jesus Christ ranks right there at the top. No one will ever be able to truly see life through God"s Eyes until they have lived for some time in a deep abiding relationship with Jesus Christ and have come to understand the grace and mercy of the Father , the truth and love of the Son and the fellowship of the Holy Spirit.

I began this book a number of years ago, actually at the time of a teaching ministry I had daily on radio called, "Abide In The Vine" - "Setting forth the abiding life in Jesus Christ." I thought I understood what it meant to abide and each day I would teach His life giving principles for living in this stress filled world. I opened each broadcast with a phrase from a song by David Engles which went, "In Him I live and move and have my being. I'm a new creature in Christ and in Christ I....... and it would fade out as i came on and said, Hi, I'm Chuck Lamka your host for Abide in the Vine. Now even through those victorious years of setting forth the principles of living life through the abiding relationship with Him I had failed to reach the depth of relationship with Him I truly desired. And since one can only give out that which one totally possesses I was unable to put into words what it means to abide in the Vine.

I understood the word of God and the teachings surrounding the abiding relationship and could have written many technical thesis on the subject and in fact did but before God would allow me to write this book He required that I would live the practical application of it. So as I dive headlong into the whitewater of the abiding life in Jesus Christ I will attempt to teach where we all should live, as my extreme athlete sons would say, "At Face Level".

We never fully understand the dangers we face nor the depth of our reliance on God's protection and intervention in our lives until we find ourselves pounded by boulders or pulled under by class V rapids. It is then that we discover whether we are all alone or actually abiding in the Vine. It is so important that we understand our commitment long before we are swept away by the violent rapids of adversity that will come our way as we navigate the river of life at face level.

A lot of years ago there was a line in a song called, "Take a Little Sonshine into Your Heart", that my wife and I would sing in vacation Bible Schools, that expresses this important principle. Now the song is talking about life in the Son of God and getting into that life fully not just wading but getting into the swim. The line that says it all is this, "The river of life is a kick and a toss, man without Jesus you sure are lost." And how true that is. This life will sweep over you to destroy you and cast you up on some beach or drown you in its' violent currents.

To many who come to Christ that River of life is a panacea. They look at the Christian life as a graceful Sunday afternoon drift down a lazy river with all the comforts of home in a powerful speed boat never encountering any problem that is more than a simple rocking of the boat. They never really get into the river of life. They just try to get by by floating on top. But to a committed Christian there are no lazy Sunday afternoon trips down that river. They have plunged deeply into the water and daily live at face level. As they do they learn how to navigate the difficulties as they face them and every twist and turn in the river brings them to a greater trust in the Lord.

In that life at face level they don't simply face life with Jesus alone but are always ready to rescue others who find themselves in trouble living at face level. So if you are one who thinks the Christian life is just a gentle ride you will never learn to abide in the Vine, but if you are ready to live life with Christ at face level I'd like to invite you to come along as we gear up for a fun but wild ride at face level as we learn what it really means to, "Abide in the Vine".

Now in the natural running rapids at face level on river boards requires a good board, helmet,mask, wet or dry suit, shin guards, flippers and safety strap as well as a great deal of strength and skill and trust in your equipment and ability and knowledge of the river and faith in God to see you through. with that said it is truly a wild ride.

Living life at face level in the river of life as you abide in the Vine requires a very special equipping and without it you can never live at face level with your Lord. If you truly desire a deep abiding relationship which can never be broken and always guarantee you will be a fruitful branch then you must daily gear up and get in the white water of life.

It would be wrong for me to assume that just because you are reading the book that you are a truly born again Christian. So the first step in our face level life of abiding in the Vine has to be a surrender of your old life and will and an entering into a new life in Christ. It is a false premise to think that all roads lead to heaven and it is also false and dangerous to think that all churches teach the truth. It is dangerous for you to trust your salvation to attending a Bible believing church or even being a tithing member of a Bible believing church. That is like jumping into a class VI rapid without even a board. I wouldn't bet on coming out alive.

God prepared the plan of redemption even before Adam and Eve sinned in the garden. When they sinned and became aware of their sin they tried to hide their sin and provide their own covering for their nakedness and to pass the blame off to others. We can't blame Adam and Eve for our sin for God says that all have sinned and come short of the glory of God. There is none righteous no not one. In Genesis 3:15 God introduces His plan for redemption and for the first time introduces the virgin birth of the Messiah or Saviour who would come to redeem mankind back to God and even though Satan would do all in his power to destroy the seed of the woman it would ultimately be that seed, [the sinless Son of God] that would crush the head of the serpent [Satan]. And then in Genesis 3:21 God begins the blood sacrifice by slaying animals and making coats of skins and clothing Adam and Eve. Now even though Adam and Eve would eventually die a physical death and when they sinned they became morally and spiritually naked before God; their death would not abrogate their sinfulness. It could only be by the substitutionary death of a pure sinless animal without spot or blemish pointing forward to the sinless Lamb of God [Jesus Christ] who takes away the sin of the world that that could happen. God's plan of redemption weaves a portrait of Christ and His involvement with His creation from Genesis through Revelation.

Years ago, when my sons first began running whitewater at face level they were doing it without proper equipment, [having taken a page from their stupid father's life], they ran the rapids on inner-tubes. Had it not been for their Heavenly Father's protection they might have been seriously injured or dead. In the same way many of God's children attempt to navigate the river of life with improper equipment and if it were not for the Lord's love and mercy and desire that none would perish they would die and go into hell without ever having a chance to receive the Saviour.

God in His mercy set the plan of redemption into operation the minute His first children sinned. The plan of redemption was actually set up before creation but instituted the moment sin entered the world. Now Adam and Eve, like so many of God's creation today, when confronted with their sin quickly blamed others. Eve said it was the serpent, 'he beguiled me' and Adam said, 'it's not my fault, the woman You gave me caused me to sin'. [paraphrase]. The blame game will keep many from ever turning from their sin to a forgiving loving God. And like all who fail to repent and turn to Christ and become washed clean by the blood of the Lamb, Adam and Eve tried to create their   own religion with it's means of redemption called fig leaf redemption but God saw right through it. There was no way this was able to cover their nakedness. No man can save himself or cover his own sin. All have sinned and come short of the glory of God and none can survive the river of life without the saving presence of the sinless Son of God.   And there is no remission of sin without the shedding of blood. That being God's truth, He took sinless animals and shed their blood to make coverings for Adam and Eve.

The death of the animals stood as a substitutionary death by ones sinless, for the sinners, and this pointed forward to the ultimate sacrifice of the Son of God. In Exodus, God instituted the passover as he had Moses lead His people out of Egypt, where they had been in slavery for four hundred years. It was here that God introduced the principle of the covering of the shed blood protecting from death all those who had placed the blood of the sacrificial lamb on the lintel and doorposts. At the same time God introduces the importance of totally identifying with the death of the sacrifice in requiring the eating of all of it that night with the unleavened bread [uncorrupted] and bitter herbs revealing the importance of our total involvement with the death of Christ, His sinless broken body and the bitterness of the occasion. Exodus 12:7-14.

Now I'm not going to take the time to cover every scripture in every book of the Bible that are part of this great tapestry of the portrait of our Lord and Saviour but I do want to look at a few. In Leviticus 17:11 we read, "For the life of the flesh is in the blood; and I have given it to you upon the altar to make an atonement for your souls; for it is the blood that maketh an atonement for the soul." The shedding of the life of a sinless one both covers and atones for the sins of the guilty one who receives it. Then in the book of Joshua we again see a different part of the beautiful tapestry painted of our Lord through that scarlet thread of redemption. Here we see that covering and atonement reaching out to one outside of God's chosen people like most of us. Rahab, a sinful woman and a Gentile chose to put her trust and faith in the eternal God and that faith had come by the hearing of the Word. Look at Joshua 2:9-19. "And she said unto the men, I know that the Lord hath given you the land, and that your terror is fallen upon us, and that all the inhabitants of the land faint because of you. For we have heard how the Lord dried up the water of the Red Sea for you, when ye came out of Egypt; and what ye did unto the two kings of the Amorites, that were on the other side Jordan, Sihon and Og. whom ye utterly destroyed. And as soon as we heard these things, our hearts did melt, neither did there remain any more courage in any man, because of you; for the Lord your God, He is God in heaven above, and in earth beneath. Now therefore, I pray you, swear unto me by the Lord, since I have showed you kindness, that ye will also shew kindness unto my father's house, and give me a true token: And that ye will save my father, and my mother, and my brethren and my sisters and all that they have, and deliver our lives from death. And the men answered her, our life for yours if ye utter not this our business and it shall be, when the Lord hath given us the land, that we will deal kindly and truly with thee. Then she let them down by a cord through the window: for her house was upon the town wall, and she dwelt upon the wall. And she said unto them. Get you to the mountain lest the pursuers meet you; and hide yourselves there three days until the pursuers be returned; and afterward may ye go your way. And the men said unto her. We will be blameless of this our oath which thou hast made us swear. Behold, when we come into the land, thou shalt bind this line of scarlet thread in the window which thou didst let us down by: and thou shalt bring thy father, and thy mother, and thy brethren, and all thy father's household, home unto thee. And it shall be that whosoever shall go out of the doors of thy house into the street, his blood shall be upon his head, and we will be guiltless: and whosoever shall be with thee in the house, his blood shall be on our heads if any hand be upon him."

That scarlet thread again represented the blood covering to all who would come under it showing salvation was extended to all who would believe. And because of Rahab's faith in the true and living God, God allowed this forgiven sinful Gentile woman to be in the linage of the Messiah [Matthew 1;5, "Salmon begat Boaz of Rahab"] thus adding to the intricate workings of the tapestry of the portrait of our Lord. Rahab was Davids great grandmother.

In Isaiah 52:13 through chapter 53 we are introduced to the sublime purpose of the scarlet thread of redemption as the heart of our tapestry is woven in the prophetic description of our suffering Saviour and the magnificent meaning of His suffering and death and all it provided for mankind. "Behold My servant shall deal prudently, He shall be exalted and extolled and be very high. As many were astonied at Thee; His visage was marred more than any man, and His form more than the sons of men: So shall He sprinkle many nations; the kings shall shut their mouths at Him: for that which had not been told them they shall see; and that which they had not heard shall they consider. Who hath believed our report? and to whom is the arm of the Lord revealed? For He shall grow up before Him as a tender plant, and as a root out of a dry ground; He hath no form nor comeliness; and when we shall see Him, there is no beauty that we should desire Him. He is despised and rejected of men; a man of sorrows and acquainted with grief; and we hid as it were our faces from Him; He was despised and we esteemed Him not. Surely He hath borne our griefs and carried our sorrows; yet we did esteem Him stricken, smitten of God, and afflicted. But He was wounded for our transgressions, He was bruised for our iniquities: the chastisement of our peace was upon Him: and with His stripes we are healed. All we like sheep have gone astray; We have turned everyone to his own way; and the Lord hath laid on Him the iniquity of us all. He was oppressed, and He was afflicted, yet He opened not His mouth: He is brought as a lamb to the slaughter, and as sheep before His shearers is dumb, so He openeth not His mouth: He was taken from prison and from judgement: and who shall declare His generation? for He was cut off out of the land of the living: for the transgression of My people was He stricken. And He made His grave with the wicked, and with the rich in His death; because He had done no violence, neither was any deceit in His mouth. Yet it pleased the Lord to bruise Him; He hath put Him to grief; when thou shalt make His soul an offering for sin, He shall see His seed, He shall prolong His days, and the pleasures of the Lord shall prosper in His hand. He shall see the travail of His soul, and shall be satisfied: by His knowledge shall My righteous servant justify many; for He shall bear their iniquities. Therefore will I divide Him a portion with the great, and He shall divide the spoil with the strong; because He hath poured out His soul unto death: and He was numbered with the transgressors; and He bare the sin of many, and made intercession for the transgressors."

Isaiah's prophesy of the coming Messiah, the Saviour of the world, was a clear and exact picture of the suffering Christ who not only provided deliverance and salvation for all mankind through His shed blood, being the pure and spotless lamb of God who took our punishment upon His back and died for us but He also provided healing of all kinds by His broken body, for by His stripes we are healed. The extent of those 39 stripes upon His back should not be minimized. The Roman soldiers used what became known as a cat of nine tails, which was a leather whip with nine strips of rawhide with pieces of metal and glass and stone imbedded in each. When they struck His back with every lash they would all cut into His flesh. Each lash would carve the flesh deeper and deeper until His back was nothing but an open wound.

Jesus knew what was coming but because of the joy set before Him and His love for His creation He willingly lay down His life and became sin for man that by His substitutionary death and resurrection we could attain unto eternal life and receive forgiveness for our sins and know fellowship with God.

Now there are many other passages such as Psalm 22 which continue to weave the portrait of Christ and His suffering for man that we could look at but my point is not simply to look at the Scarlet Thread of Redemption from one view but when you have time read the 22nd Psalm and you will see the exact description of the crucifixion of Christ and crucifixion did not exist as a means of punishment when the Holy Spirit moved upon David to write that Psalm. It was created by the Romans many years later. So now let's take a look at the portrait as it is continued to be woven in the New Testament.

In Matthew 26:26-28 we read these words, "And as they were eating, Jesus took bread and blessed it and brake it and gave it to the disciples, and said, take eat; this is My body. And He took the cup, and gave thanks and gave it to them, saying Drink ye all of it; For this is My blood of the New Testament, which is shed for many for the remission of sins." Luke adds the words in Luke 22:19, "..........this do in remembrance of Me."

When Jesus introduced what has become known as the Lord's supper He was celebrating His last Passover and explaining the true meaning of those things done in the Passover to the disciples showing clearly that He is the true Passover lamb and the broken bread and that it was only His shed blood and broken body that provided redemption. The followers of Jesus had celebrated many Passovers and three with Jesus. They had heard Him refer to His death and resurrection. They heard Him refer to Himself as the true bread which came down from Heaven and that in order to have any part in Him they must eat of Him and drink of Him. They had heard John the Baptist refer to Him as the Lamb of God that takes away the sin of the world but they still didn't comprehend and even now as He speaks clearly of His death they are unable to grasp what it is He is saying. It was only after His death and resurrection that they were able to comprehend the true meaning of partaking of His death and resurrection. Here He was not speaking in a literal physical sense but in a spiritual where we would understand that we must fully identify with Him in His suffering and death and resurrection in order to understand what it means to abide in Him.

We are forbidden in God's word to eat or drink the blood of an animal for the life is in the blood and it was the shedding of blood that provided forgiveness. Jesus was saying that it was through His shed blood that we have life and we need to identify with and partake of His life. As we continue in this thought in order to get a clearer picture look at John's gospel in chapter 6 verses 53-58. "Then

Jesus said unto them, Verily verily, I say unto you, Except ye eat the flesh of the Son of man and drink His blood, ye have no life in you. Whoso eateth My flesh, and drinketh my blood, hath eternal life and I will raise him up at the last day. For My flesh is meat indeed, and my blood is drink indeed. He that eateth My flesh and drinketh My blood dwelleth in Me and I in Him. As the living Father hath sent me, and I live by the Father, so he that eateth Me even he shall live by Me. This is that bread which came down from heaven: not as your fathers did eat manna and are dead: he that eateth of this bread shall live for ever."

This was hard for His Disciples to comprehend for they were at this point having a hard time receiving the fact of His divine origin and the importance of fully identifying with the gruesome death He would soon face for all mankind. Even today looking back at the cross it is difficult to fully understand the vital importance of our complete absorption into all He underwent for us and if you attempt to remove the cross or our identification and participation in it you have a Christ-less Christianity and that is no Christianity at all. To identify with Christ totally means we deny ourselves and daily identify with His suffering and are willing to be crucified with Him as Mark recorded in his gospel in Mark8:34. "And when He had called the people unto Him with His disciples also, He said unto them, Whosoever will come after Me, let him deny himself and take up his cross and follow Me."

To be a true disciple of Christ and abide in the Vine means we must fully immerse ourselves in everything He did at face level It is recorded in John 19:33-37 after He had become sin for mankind and suffered and died for us they pierced His side with a spear and blood and water poured out fulfilling the necessity of the shedding of blood for without it there is no forgiveness for sin. "But when they came to Jesus and saw that He was dead already, they brake not His legs: But one of the soldiers with a spear pierced His side, and forthwith came there out blood and water. And he that saw it bare record and his record is true: and he knoweth that he saith true, that ye might believe. For these things were done that the scripture should be fulfilled, a bone of Him shall not be broken. and another scripture saith, they shall look on Him whom they pierced."

Then in Romans we look at our portrait of Christ's redemptive act through His shed blood and what it means to us. Romans 3:23-26, "For all have sinned and come short of the glory of God; Being justified freely by His grace through the redemption that is in Christ Jesus: Whom God hath set forth to be a propitiation through faith in His blood, to declare His righteousness for the remission of sins that are past, through the forbearance of God; to declare, I say, at this time His righteousness: that He might be just, and the justifier of him which believeth in Jesus." And Romans 5:8-11 says, "But God commendeth His Love toward us, in that, while we were yet sinners, Christ died for us. Much more then being now justified by His blood we shall be saved from wrath through Him. For if, when we were enemies, we were reconciled to God by the death of His Son, much more, being reconciled, we shall be saved by His life. And not only so, but we also joy in God through our Lord Jesus Christ by whom we have now received the atonement."

The first step in our abiding life in Jesus Christ and learning to live in that life at face level is accepting the free gift of salvation and eternal life which our Lord provided by His shed blood on the Cross, It was then He took our punishment for us and by our acceptance of that and our total identification of all He did and all He is that we hear the judgement against us of not guilty. This becomes our first step into the exciting life in the river of life as we begin to trust Christ to lead us and guide us through the calm waters and the raging storms we will face at face level abiding in Him.

I want to add to our portrait of Christ a few more scriptures that pertain to our living at face level the abiding life, now that we have accepted Him as our Lord and Saviour, so look at II Corinthians 5:14-21, "For the love of Christ constraineth us: because we thus judge, that if one died for all, then were all dead; And that He died for all that they which should live should not henceforth live unto themselves, but unto Him which died for them, and rose again. Wherefore henceforth know we no man after the flesh: yea, though we have known Christ after the Flesh, yet now henceforth know we Him no more. Therefore if any man be in Christ, he is a new creature: old things are passed away; behold, all things are become new. and all things are of God, who hath given to us the ministry of reconciliation; to wit, that God was in Christ reconciling the world unto Himself, not imputing their trespasses unto them; and hath committed unto us the word of reconciliation. Now then we are ambassadors for Christ, as though God did beseech you by us: we pray you in Christ's stead, be ye reconciled to God. For He hath made Him to be sin for us, who knew no sin; that we might be made the righteousness of God in Him."

We need to realize that as we accept what Christ did as our substitute in dying for us that we are dead [the old nature] with Christ and now live in Christ [a new creation]. So now we need to live unto Him as a spiritual being in a physical body and not live after the desires of the flesh which was crucified with Christ. He has put us into right relationship with the Father and we now put on the righteousness of God in Him.

Then in Colossians 1:9-12 we get a real glimpse of what Christ has done for us. For this cause we also, since the day we heard it, do not cease to pray for you, and to desire that ye might be filled with the knowledge of His will in all wisdom and spiritual understanding; That ye might walk worthy of the Lord unto all pleasing, being fruitful in every good work, and increasing in the knowledge of God: Strengthened with all might according to His glorious power, unto all patience and long-suffering with joyfulness; giving thanks unto the Father, which hath made us meet to be partakers of the inheritance of the saints in light: Who hath delivered us from the power of darkness, and hath translated us into the kingdom of his dear Son; In whom we have redemption through His blood, even the forgiveness of sins: Who is the image of the invisible God, the firstborn of every creature: For by Him were all things created, that are in heaven, and that are in earth, visible and invisible, whether they be thrones, or dominions, or principalities or powers: all things were created by Him, and for Him: And He is before all things, and by Him all things consist. and He is the head of the body, the church: who is the beginning, the firstborn from the dead; that in all things He might have the preeminence. For it pleased the Father that in him should all the fulness dwell; And having made peace through the blood of His cross, by Him to reconcile all things unto Himself: by Him, I say, whether they be things in earth or things in heaven. And you that were sometime alienated and enemies in your mind by wicked works, yet now hath He reconciled, in the body of His flesh through death, to present you holy and unblameable and unreproveable in His sight." And verse 23a says, "if ye continue in the faith grounded and settled and be not moved away from the hope of the gospel which ye have heard, and which was preached to every creature which is under heaven;................"

Now let's look at this at face level and see what it really means to us as we learn to abide in Christ. It is as we set our eyes on the Master and begin to follow Him in the river of life that we gain wisdom and spiritual understanding as we gain the knowledge of His will which includes being filled with the Spirit and as we live in the Spirit and walk in the Spirit His personal will for each of our lives will become clear. You can refuse His will and go your own way but the journey will not be a pleasant one at face level. As we live in Christ we are to walk worthy of Him, please Him and become fruitful and gain greater knowledge of God. As you abide in Him every movement He makes in that river of life you will make and you will gain strength through His power. You will learn patience and endure long-suffering as you navigate the dangerous and difficult rapids of life and with Him you will endure those things with true joy fully understanding as you go through the difficult times what it means when the word says that because of the joy set before Him, Jesus endured the cross and the shame. As we endure we can thank the Father for seeing us through all the rapids we can't handle alone knowing that He has made us partakers of the inheritance that is Christ's that He shares with all the saints delivering us out of darkness into His marvelous light. Our lives are now hid in Christ in His Kingdom which He purchased by His shed blood as He also purchased and redeemed us from sin and brought forgiveness. As we learn to abide in Christ we need to understand that He is not only the image of the invisible God but that all things were made by Him, and for Him, both on earth and in heaven, whether seen or unseen. Every kingdom, every dominion, every power and every problem, every obstacle, every boulder and every rapid we face He created and He knows how to navigate each twist and turn we face.

He is the head of the body and we are each members of that body which is the church and it is He and He alone that is to have preeminence. We are as members of His body and disciples of Christ to be like our master but we will never be the master. Every twist and turn we face will give us a greater understanding of what it means to truly abide. All the fulness of God dwells in the Son and the Son has made peace with His entire creation by His shed blood on the cross as He reconciled all things in Heaven and earth unto Himself and now He is at work daily to perfect each of us in order to present us holy and without blame unto the Father, and that He will do, if we live with Him at face level continuing in faith [totally believing and trusting] and as we become grounded and settled in our relationship with our Lord, and not move away from the hope of the truth of the gospel, [the good news of the word of God.] In Hebrews 13:12-15 we read, "Wherefore Jesus also, that He might sanctify the people with His own blood, suffered without the gate. Let us go forth therefore unto Him without the camp, bearing His reproach. For here have we no continuing city, but we seek one to come. By Him therefore let us offer the sacrifice of praise to God continually, that is the fruit of our lips giving thanks to His name."

As we establish a deep abiding relationship with Christ we will discover a greater hatred from the world but we need to bear His reproach realizing that this earth is not our home and that we seek a city whose builder and maker is God. So let us as living sacrifices offer the sacrifice of praise unto God continually which is the fruit of our lips giving thanks unto His name for all He has done. The further along the river of life you travel and the greater is your understanding of God's word and God's way the stronger will be your abiding relationship and the more rapids you meet and endure and navigate through with Christ the more things you will have to praise Him for.

In 1 Peter 1:13-19 Peter admonishes us, because of the shed blood of Jesus Christ, to leave the things of the world and the lusts of the flesh and to be holy for He is holy. "Wherefore gird up the loins of your mind, be sober, and hope to the end for the grace that is to be brought unto you at the revelation of Jesus Christ; As obedient children, not fashioning yourselves according to the former lusts in your ignorance: But as He which hath called you is holy, so be ye holy in all manner of conversation; Because it is written,, Be ye holy; for I am holy. And if ye call on the Father, Who without respect of persons judgeth according to ever man's work; pass the time of your sojourning here in fear: Forasmuch as ye know that ye were not redeemed with corruptible things, as silver and gold, from your vain conversation received by tradition from your fathers; But with the precious blood of Christ, as of a lamb without blemish and without spot."   Our redemption and deliverance , from the slavery of this world and its aimless purposes come not of money but by the precious blood of Christ who was pure and sinless and holy in every way. Now as we learn to live at face level with Him we need to separate ourselves from the useless vanities of the old life and live a holy life. Our entire conduct or manner of action and speech should be holy. If we are going to grow in our abiding relationship with Christ to where we are bringing forth spiritual life then we must put on His righteousness, walk in His light and be holy. We cannot do it outside of Christ. We are not capable of doing that on our own. I want to look at one more scripture in the portrait of Christ woven in scripture by the scarlet thread of redemption before moving on to chapter II. So let's look at the last book of the Bible as John records the vision he receives from Jesus and address the the seven churches of Asia in Revelation 1:5-8. "And from Jesus Christ, who is the faithful witness, and the first begotten of the dead, and the prince of the kings of the earth. Unto Him that loved us, and washed us from our sins in His own blood, and hath made us kings and priests unto God and His Father: to Him be glory and dominion for ever and ever. Amen. Behold , He cometh with clouds; and every eye shall see Him, and they also which pierced Him: and all kindreds of the earth shall wail because of Him. Even so, Amen. I am the Alpha and Omega, the beginning and the ending, saith the Lord, which is, and which was, and which is to come, the almighty." The tapestry would be incomplete if it didn't show our victorious Saviour coming again and ruling in power but as the angles said unto the disciples of Jesus as they stood gazing into space as He was taken up into heaven [Acts 1:11], ".......Ye men of Galilee, why stand ye gazing up into heaven? This same Jesus, which is taken up from you into heaven, shall so come in like manner as ye have seen Him go into heaven." So also we are told in Revelation that jesus Christ, the first begotten of the dead, the King of Kings, who has made us kings and priests unto God, He who is the first and the last, the beginning and the end, the almighty is coming again, in the clouds, a victor King and every eye shall see Him when He returns that final time and will you rule and reign with Him forever? You will if you put your faith and trust in Him and live daily with Him at face level in the "River of Life".

Chapter II
"Believe Trust And Abide"

If your belief is in a far off God and your trust is in uncertainty then it is time to get wet and really learn what it means to believe, trust and abide for without the true intimate relationship with the living loving Saviour you will never be able to overcome the rapids you will face in the river of life.

To believe is much more than a simple intellectual assent that says, 'I accept that premise as real or true.' To believe in the way the word expects us to believe requires that we trust with veracity. We are so convinced in the truth of God's word and the reality and validity of every promise in God's word that we will trust Christ with everything we have and everything we are. We will do whatever He asks with no questions and no doubts. We become 'a trust'. We were purchased by the blood of Jesus Christ and as such it is for our benefit that we put our trust in Him and for His benefit and the benefit of His church that we become 'His Trust'. To truly believe means to rely; depend and have total confidence in all Christ is, says and does. it means to confidently hope in all things; to expect with total assurance the promised result in the Word of God.

There is a story I heard years ago that I have often used. I can't tell you who first originated the story or whether or not the story was true but none the less the thought is true. There was a man who would stretch a cable across between Canada and the United States above Niagara Falls where it plummets several hundred feet to the waters below and then as the crowds would gather on both sides of the falls below him to watch he would proceed to walk across the cable first in one direction and then the other.

Then he would dance across and finally take a wheelbarrow across while running and dancing. Then with the crowds rapt attention he would call down to those below and say, How many of you believe that I can put a man in the wheelbarrow and push him across the cable from America to Canada and Back?" Everyone would holler, "We believe." Then would come the next question which would be the show stopper! "Who wants to get in?" ....[NO HANDS WOULD GO UP]. They didn't truly believe in the sense God's word means for they were unwilling to trust the man with all they had and their very lives. God requires that we trust Him completely.

Can you honestly say that is where you stand in your relationship with the Lord? If you can, I applaud you! You are not far from the state of perfection that Jesus means when He says, "Be ye perfect for your heavenly Father is perfect." Before continuing on in depth, look at a few different Hebrew and Greek words which are translated abide and look at the scriptures where each is used and see what we can glean from each in coming to understand what it means to abide in the Vine or in Christ, who is the Vine. {Just a note that would be good to keep in mind is the fact that Jesus is the Word and every word in the Bible either refers to something about God and His perfection and holiness or His relationship to us, His creation.}

Depending on how the word is used it could be translated abide, abideth or abiding. The first word I want to look at is yashab . this word carries the meaning to sit down [as to ambush] [to marry and remain or to make to dwell]. It appears in Genesis and Psalms and I and II Samuel and Jeremiah. Genesis 24:55 reads, "And her brother and her mother said, Let the damsel abide with us for a few days, at the least ten: after that she shall go." In this situation for Rebecca to remain where she was would have placed her in a situation that would have kept her from the abiding relationship God had designed. If we are not careful we can find ourselves ambushed into an abiding relationship which may look right on the outset but keep us from abiding in the Vine. In Genesis 44:33 we read, "Now therefore, I pray thee, let thy servant abide instead of the lad a bondman to my lord; and let the lad go up with his brethren." Judah was willing to make himself a sacrifice and become a slave so Benjamin could return to his father. Are we willing to sacrifice ourselves so others can come to abide with the heavenly Father? Pause and think about it. In Psalm 61:7 David lays out the true purpose of abiding, "He shall abide before God forever: O prepare mercy and truth, which may preserve him."

In other words David was saying, O God let me sit before You as in a marriage relationship forever and may your mercy and truth protect, guard and keep me in that relationship. This is the exact meaning we are looking for, built in truth and unable to be separated!

In I Samuel Hanna speaks of the future promised relationship Samuel would have with the Lord. I Samuel 1:22, "But Hanna went not up, for she said unto her husband, I will not go up until the child be weaned, and then I will bring him, that he may appear before the Lord, and there abide for ever." Samuel was a promise of the Lord that Hanna promised to give back to the Lord to [abide], remain joined to the Lord forever and his life showed that intimate abiding relationship with God that was fruitful, prophetic and miraculous. I Samuel 5:7 shows us that the abiding relationship with God cannot take place outside of righteousness. If we are not walking with God and are outside of the fold and worshiping other things; we will discover that God's presence cannot dwell with ungodliness. "And when the men of Ashdod saw that it was so they said, The Ark of God of Israel shall not abide with us; for His hand is sore upon us, and upon Dagon our god." We can have no other gods before Him.

What are the idols in your life? Wife? Husband? Children? Money? Job? Prestige? Pride? What ever it is that keeps you from being totally sold out to God has to go or you will never know the true abiding relationship that is necessary to be all God wants you to be.

The abiding relationship is also designed for your protection. In I Samuel 19:2 we see Jonathan's concern for David's safety making him dwell and hide in a secret place. And David tells us in Psalms, speaking of the Lord, "Thou art my hiding place." Even though David was hiding in a physical place he knew it was only the Lord who was his protector and hiding place. "But Jonathan, Saul's son delighted much in David saying, Saul my father seeketh to kill thee: now therefore I pray thee take heed to thyself until the morning and abide in a secret place and hide thyself." If we abide in Christ we understand the words of David when he says, "Thou art my hiding place. Thou shalt preserve me from trouble." What a wonderful thing to know that we need to {"Fear Not"}. God will hide us from the pursuit of our enemies.

God may place you in a position of leadership and design a full and rich future for you but because of fear of situations or things or people coming against you, you find yourself abiding in the wrong place. This was David's problem when pursued by Saul he first abides in the enemies camp, then a cave; but when the prophet Gad tells him to abide not in the Hold but return to Judah he begins to face his enemies head on at face level and discovers afresh the guidance and protection and victory in the abiding relationship with the Lord.

If you look at Psalm 91 where the word for abide is the Hebrew word luwn - which gives the idea of stopping in a place over night for protection. In other words we can run to Him to hide. He is there to receive you. Here you will see spelled out God's divine protection for all those who take up residency in the secret place of the most high and remain fixed, abiding under the shadow of 'El Shadday or God Almighty'. Both King James and the Amplified use the word secret place while some others say shelter but the meaning is a place of protection hidden or unknown by those not there. Take a close look at each and every verse and then ask yourself if that is the protection and divine health you have come to know and if not are you in need of entering into that relationship? "He that dwelleth in the secret place of of the most high shall abide under the shadow of the Almighty, I will say of the Lord, He is my refuge and my fortress: my God; in Him will I trust. Surely He shall deliver thee from the snare of the fowler, and from the noisome pestilence. He shall cover thee with His feathers, and under His wings shalt thou trust: His truth shall be thy shield and buckler. Thou shalt not be afraid for the terror by night; nor for the arrow that flieth by day; nor for the pestilence that walketh in darkness; nor for the destruction that wasteth at noonday. A thousand shall fall at thy side and ten thousand at thy right hand; but it shall not come nigh thee. Only with thine eyes shalt thou behold and see the reward of the wicked. Because thou hast made the Lord, which is my refuge, even the Most High, thy habitation; There shall no evil befall thee, neither shall any plague come nigh thy dwelling. For He shall give His angels charge over thee, to keep the in all thy ways. They shall bear thee up in their hands, lest thou dash thy foot against a stone. Thou shalt tread upon the lion and adder: the young lion and the dragon shalt thou trample under feet. Because He hath set His love upon me, therefore will I deliver him: I will set him on high, because he hath known My name. He shall call upon Me, and I will answer him and honor him. With long life will I satisfy him, and show him My salvation."

There are certain requirements to abiding in the tabernacle and living in God's holy hill or the true resting place and presence of God or literally abiding in God or in Christ. Look at Psalm 15. This is how it reads, "Lord, who shall abide in Thy tabernacle? Who shall dwell in Thy holy hill? He that walketh uprightly, and worketh righteousness,and speaketh the truth in his heart. He that backbiteth not with his tongue, nor doeth evil to his neighbor, nor taketh up a reproach against his neighbor. In whose eyes a vile person is condemned; but he hounoureth them that fear the Lord. He that sweareth to his own hurt, and changeth not. He that putteth not out his money to usury, nor taketh reward against the innocent. He that doeth these things shall never be moved." This is the word in Hebrew for abide meaning to turn aside and stand in awe.

David adds to this list in Psalms 24:3-5, "Who shall ascend into the hill of the Lord? or who shall stand in His holy place? He that hath clean hands, and a pure heart; who hath not lifted up his soul unto vanity, nor sworn deceitfully. He shall receive the blessing from the Lord, and righteousness from the God of his salvation."

There is great blessing in a true abiding relationship in the Lord but it means a separation from the things of the world unto a life of holiness. Look with me at David's list and see how you are doing:

1) Walk uprightly - To walk and live one's life in and before God in a morally correct and just manner being ethical in all dealings.
2) Work righteousness - To exert one's self both physically and mentally in moral purity and justice in order to obtain the same and bring others to a state of righteousness.
3) Speak the truth in your heart - Meditate and practice that which is exact, actual and honest in your heart; set your heart on the Truth, [Christ is the Truth].

4) Does not backbite with his tongue - Does not use one's tongue to cut, belittle, slander, defame or cause harm or shame to another.
5) Don't do evil to your neighbor - Don't act as a villain and do wickedness or work mischief, wrong, or be vicious, causing harm, injury, misfortune or disaster to befall your neighbor. [remember who Jesus says your neighbor is].
6) Don't take up a reproach against your neighbor - Don't misuse, deceive, betray, mistreat, harm, scold, berate, vilify, insult, libel, slander or violate your neighbor.
7) Despise that which is vile - One who loathes, disdains, abhors, hates and dislikes the actions of one who is vile, dirty, foul, nasty, slimy, vicious and villainous or morally delinquent.
8) Honors those that fear the Lord - Respects, reverences, regards, esteems, trusts, praises and gives recognition to those that tremble before, reverence, respect and worship the Lord God.
9) Sweareth to his own hurt and changes not - Bound by an oath or promise that cause one hurt, mental pain, anguish, annoyance, damage, suffering or injury whether mental, physical or financial and stands by the promise.
10) Does not charge usury - Does not charge excess interest and charges no interest to the poor nor to his brethren - Does not charge others that which is more than the law allows or what would be considered beyond reason by a reasonable person.
11) Does not take a bribe against the innocent - Does not take anything of value or take advantage; corrupt, entice, seduce, or sway in opposition to or contrary to the innocent [one who is guiltless, sinless, blameless, unblemished, honest, pure, naive, harmless and inoffensive].
12) Has clean hands - Is a person of integrity who is honest in all his doings and above reproach.

13) A pure heart - One who's heart is set on God; is unstained, unblemished, virtuous and chaste and is not corrupted by the things of the world. The dross has been removed and that which is left is pure gold.
14) Not lifted up his soul to vanity - One who has not pridefully elevated his being to emptiness or things without purpose or that which is false.
15) Not Sworn deceitfully - Does not make a vow or promise or assert, state, or testify with treachery, cunning or falsehood to cheat, mislead. swindle, hoodwink or delude.

If you can honestly say that is you then you are truly blessed and your life should abound with miracles.

The next word is the word quwm which we find in Nahum 1:6 and which carries some interesting meanings. The word quwm means to rise, abide, accomplish, continue or rise again, strengthen and succeed. Nahum 1:6 reads, "Who can stand before His indignation and who can abide in the fierceness of His anger? His fury is poured out like fire, and the rocks are thrown down by Him." Nahum makes a strong point that nothing can withstand the judgement of God, and then in verse 7 he shows God's goodness and protection for those who trust and abide in Him. Look for a minute at verse 6 this way. "Who can stand before God's indignation and who can [abide, rise up, continue in, endure and rise again and succeed or accomplish anything] in the fierceness of God's anger? His fury is poured out like fire and the rocks are thrown down by Him." None can abide before God if they are facing His judgement but if we trust and abide in Him we will rise up and rise again, succeed and accomplish that which God gives us to do and endure to the end. In Malachi 3:2-3 we get even a broader view of what it means to abide as Malachi asks the question, "But who may abide the day of His coming? and who shall stand when He appeareth? for He is like a refiner's fire, and like fullers sope: and He shall sit as a refiner and purifier of silver: and He shall purify the sons of Levi, and purge them as gold and silver, that they may offer unto the Lord an offering in righteousness."

If we are going to abide in the Lord we can expect to go through the fire of purification and be purged of all unrighteousness. He will not allow us to abide in Him and retain any of the stench of the world. The dross will be removed or we will not abide. The word in Malachi is the Hebrew word kuwl - to keep in, to maintain, to bear, comprehend, nourish, and provide sustenance.

So outside of enduring and allowing the purification of our lives we will be unable to abide or maintain a relationship in God's presence. We will be unable to bear His coming and the spiritual nourishment we will not receive. We cannot even comprehend the magnitude of what that day of His coming will mean. If we fail to pass through the fire of His purifying we will drown in the rapids of our own foolishness and sorrow.

In the New Testament we find several words translated abide which we shall look at , and while there are other Hebrew words translated abide we will leave them for later. The first I want to look at in Greek is the word mino. This is the word most often used and it carries the meaning of permanence. We come to understand that to abide means to stay in a given place, state of mind, relationship or expectancy; to continue, dwell, endure, be patient, remain, stand and tarry there.

We find this word used in Matthew, Mark, Luke and many times in John. We also see it in Acts, the letters of Paul to the Corinthians, Philippians, Timothy and in Hebrews, I Peter and I John so lets look at a few. In Matthew 10 Jesus sends forth the twelve disciples and instructs them on carrying out His work. And in verse 11 He tells them to find someone worthy in each town they enter and abide with them until they would leave that city or town. "And into whatsoever city or town ye shall enter, enquire who in it is worthy; and there abide till ye go hence." In other words find a righteous individual whom you can trust and remain with them while you are going about doing the work of God. Salute the home and bring God's peace and blessing to that home. If none are found worthy don't abide in that town for any reason. In Luke 19:5 we read, "And when Jesus came to the place, He looked up, and saw him, and said unto him. Zacchaeus, make haste and come down; for today I must abide at thy house." Zacchaeus wanted to see Jesus but Jesus wanted to abide in a permanent sense. In verse 6 it says, "And He made haste, and came down and received Him joyfully." and in verses 9-10 Jesus says, "...........This day is salvation come to this house, forasmuch as he is a son of Abraham. For the son of man is come to seek and to save that which was lost."

It is a permanent relationship the Lord desires with all of us. In Luke 24:13-36 we read, "And behold, two of them went that day to a village called Emmaus, which was from Jerusalem about threescore furlongs. And they talked together of all these things which had happened. And it came to pass that, while they communed together and reasoned, Jesus, Himself drew near and went with them. But their eyes were holden that they should not know Him. And He said unto them, What manner of communication are these that ye have one to another as ye walk, and are sad? And the one of them whose name was Cleopus answering said unto Him, art Thou only a stranger in Jerusalem, and hast not known the things which are come to pass there in these days? And He said unto them, What things? And they said unto Him, concerning Jesus of Nazareth, which was a prophet mighty in deed and word before God and all the people: And how the chief priests and our rulers delivered Him to be condemned to death, and have crucified Him. But we trusted that it had been He which should have redeemed Israel: and beside all this, today is the third day since these things were done. Yea, and certain women also of our company made us astonished, which were early at the sepulchre; And when they found not His body, they come, saying, that they had also seen a vision of angels, which said that He was alive, And certain of them which were with us went to the sepulchre, and found it even as the women had said: but Him they saw not. Then He said unto them, O fools and slow of heart to believe all that the prophets have spoken: Ought not Christ to have suffered these things and to enter into His glory? And beginning at Moses and all the prophets, He expounded unto them in all the scriptures the things concerning Himself. And they drew nigh unto the village, whither they went: and He made as though He would have gone further. But they constrained Him saying. Abide with us: for it is toward evening, and the day is far spent. And He went in to tarry with them. And it came to pass, as He sat at meat with them, He took bread and blessed it and brake and gave to them. And their eyes were opened, and they knew Him; and He vanished out of their sight. And they said one to another, Did not our heart burn within us by the way, and while He opened to us the scriptures? And they rose up the same hour, and returned to Jerusalem and found the eleven gathered together and them that were with them, saying, The Lord is risen indeed and hath appeared to Simon. And they told what things were done in the way, and how He was known of them in breaking of bread. And as they thus spake, Jesus Himself stood in the midst of them, and saith unto them, Peace be unto you."

Jesus walked with them and talked with them and His presence caused their hearts to burn within to the point where hey invited Him to abide with them but His intention at that time was only to tarry awhile. But when their eyes were opened and they knew Him and He vanished, all they wanted was to find Him and abide in His presence and immediately set out for Jerusalem even though it was night and , yes, Jesus met them there. Have your eyes been opened to see the living Lord? If they have then you too will want to abide always in His presence.

In John 12:46 we read these words of Jesus, "I am come a light into the world, that whosoever believeth on me should not abide in darkness." Jesus, who is the Word of God came proclaiming the word of God as John tells us in John 1:3-4, "All things were made by Him and without Him was not anything made that was made. In Him was life and the life was the light of men." It is in that relationship of an abiding life in Jesus Christ that we receive the light within and do not remain in darkness or as Strong's says, obscurity or separation from light where everything is evil or morally deprived. Jesus Came to turn on the switch that we might truly see the light and dwell in the light and know God. Then Jesus says in John 14:15-17 the following. "If ye love Me, keep My commandments and I will pray the Father, and He shall give you another comforter, that He may abide with you forever:Even the Spirit of truth; whom the world cannot receive because it seeth Him not neither knoweth Him: but ye know Him; for He dwelleth with you, and shall be in you." Jesus says if we love Him and if we keep His commandments the Father will send the Holy Spirit to abide [permanently remain] within us forever. Please notice it requires something of us. Do you love the Lord? Do you love God with all your heart,soul, mind and strength and your fellow man as yourself? Does He come first in everything and in every way? Are you committed to living that abiding life with Christ in the river of life at face level? [Selah] STOP AND THINK ABOUT IT!

Then in the 15th chapter of John Jesus spells out in detail what it means to abide [remain permanently] in the Vine so let's look at it verse by verse. John 15:1-8 reads, "I am the true vine, and My Father is the husbandman. Every branch in Me that beareth not fruit He taketh away and every branch that beareth fruit He purgeth it that it may bring forth more fruit. Now ye are clean through the word which I have spoken unto you. Abide in Me and I in you as the branch cannot bear fruit of itself, except it abide in the vine, no more can ye except ye abide in Me. I am the vine, ye are the branches. He that abideth in Me, and I in him, the same bringeth forth much fruit; for without Me ye can do nothing. If a man abide not in Me he is cast forth as a branch and is withered and men gather them and cast them into the fire and they are burned. If ye abide in Me, and I in you, ye shall ask what ye will and it shall be done unto you. Herein is My Father glorified, that ye bear much fruit, so shall ye be My disciples."

In these first eight verses Jesus points out the vital importance of our permanent attachment to Him and the fact that, if we don't abide in the vine we will be cut out and cast in the fire. In verse one He tells us that our Heavenly Father is the one who does the pruning. Verse two tells us that if we don't bear fruit God will remove us from the vine and if we are fruitful He will purge us or prune us so we will be more fruitful. God corrects those who are His so don't be concerned if God has you in the Woodshed, for it is for your good that you will become more fruitful which brings glory to the Father. In verse three, Jesus said that our purification, or sanctification comes through His word but realize that it is not the hearers of the word that are justified but instead the doers. Again for us to be clean requires something of us. In verse four Jesus tells us that we must abide in Him and He in us in order to be fruitful. Remember Jesus is not simply the Vine [the source of life] but also the Word. Look at it this way. Abiding in Christ requires that we are continually or permanently in fellowship with the Lord and permanently in the word of God. "Study to show yourself approved." "Meditate on the word day and night." And furthermore Christ must dwell within you and live through you so that you are guided and led of the Spirit in all things and the Word of God must be a permanent part of your life so that the light of Christ is within and there is no room for darkness. Then and only then can we be assured that out of the abundance of the heart the mouth speaks what God would have you to speak which is the truth of God. Verse five repeats the relationship because of its' dire importance and Jesus also states that without Him we are not only unfruitful but without the source of life there is nothing we can do. "Only what you do for Christ will Last." In other words what we do in our own strength is vanity, empty and useless. In verse six we are told that if we do not abide in Christ the end result is that we will be cut out of the vine like a dead branch. I'm afraid that we fail to look at the abiding life for what it really entails. Far too many people think they can walk in and out of a deep relationship with the Lord in the same way they walk in and out of the doors of a church when the truth is that, that relationship is to be permanent, 24/7. Verse seven says if that is the relationship we have, answered prayers will be what we see and live in. Then in verse eight the word tells us that our abiding relationship, which brings fruitfulness, brings glory to the Father and solidifies our relationship as Jesus true disciples.

The next three verses express the love and joy experienced in and through that ongoing relationship. John 15:9-11 reads, "As the Father hath loved Me, so have I loved you: continue ye in My love. If ye keep My commandments ye shall abide in My love ; even as I have kept My Father's commandments and abide in His love. These things have I spoken unto you, that My joy might remain in you, and that your joy might be full." Experiencing the love of the Father through the love of the Son as a lasting abiding love relationship filled with the joy of the Lord, which brings a full lasting joy to your life comes only as you keep the commandments of the Lord in the same way that Jesus did everything the Father gave Him to do. We need to remember that Jesus basically broke down those commandments to two! Which are these;[Love God with all your heart, soul, mind and strength and love your neighbor as yourself]. Doing this encompasses all the law and prophets. In this way God will always come first and you will never do harm to others.

The abiding life brings a life of joy. As we travel the river of life with Christ as our guide there is a joy we experience even among the rapids we face and go through all of the challenges we face. In the physical sense of running rivers at face level , if you have a guide the experience can really be a joyful one even when you face some challenging whitewater.

In verses twelve through twenty-two Jesus, as our guide in the river of life, gives us instructions on navigating that river and the importance of our relationship one to another. If the instructions given as you run physical rivers with others aren't heeded you can find yourself in troubled waters or endanger other's lives. The same is true as we navigate the white water of the river of life. The following verses read this way, "This is My commandment, that ye love one another as I have loved you. Greater love hath no man than this, that a man lay down his life for his friends. Ye are my friends if ye do whatsoever I command you. Henceforth I call you not servants; for the servant knoweth not what his lord doeth; but I have called you friends; for all things that I have heard of My Father I have made known unto you. Ye have not chosen Me, but I have chosen you, and ordained you, that ye should go and bring forth fruit and that your fruit should remain: that whatsoever ye shall ask of the Father in My name, He may give it you. These things I command you, that ye love one another. If the world hate you, ye know that it hated Me before it hated you. If ye were of the world, the world would love his own: but because ye are not of the world but I have chosen you out of the world, therefore the world hateth you. Remember the word that I said unto you. The servant is not greater than his lord. If they have persecuted Me they will also persecute you; if they have kept My sayings, they will keep yours also. But all these things will they do unto you for My name's sake, because they know not Him that sent Me."

Jesus, our guide, as we navigate our way through the rapids we face calls us friends. He says we are truly His friends if we do all His commands. As His friends He reveals to us all the Father has spoken unto Him. Every lesson, every warning, every instruction we need He gives to us because of His great love for us. And in order for us to receive eternal life He gave His life for us.

The abiding relationship which Jesus describes as Himself being the vine [the source of carrying the flow of life] and we being the branches [that which bears fruit] was not of our choosing but of His. Whether we were a natural branch or grafted in it was by our Lord's choosing. He chose to give His life as a ransom for all mankind. We didn't choose for Him to do that. We were the reason and if we abide in the Vine we will be fruitful and live in His love and joy and love in return. Even though He chose each of us our fruitfulness and success as we live at face level depends on our choosing to heed His word, follow His commands, love one another and abide [permanently remain] in the Vine.

God ordained each of us to be fruitful but just like there are many boulders and dangerous rapids and hazards in running physical rivers there are constant dangers and obstacles we face in this life that are there to keep us from succeeding in all God has ordained for our lives.

Friends, the world will hate you and do all it can to destroy you. But remember it hated Jesus first. If you run whitewater and you heed the instructions of your guide you can safely transverse each and every rapid and maneuver your way through or around every obstacle provided he is a qualified guide familiar with the river. Remember your guide has already conquered what you are now going through and He will not allow you to be tested beyond what you can endure but will always give you a means of escape. And remember Jesus will never leave you or forsake you in your hour of need as we face the world while abiding in Him at face level.

The world would destroy us if it could but just remember that it is in Christ that you live and move and have your being and He is victorious.

Because He chose us out of the world, the world will hate us because it hates Him. The world will persecute us because it persecutes Him. We will never be greater than our master but it is His desire that we be like Him and that can only happen as we abide in the VINE.

Don't forget as we are told in I Peter 2:9, "But ye are a chosen generation a royal priesthood, an holy nation, a peculiar people; that ye should shew forth the praises of Him who hath called you out of darkness into His marvelous light."

As you believe, trust and abide you will be fruitful and victorious enjoying the joy of the Lord as you live a joyful life!

Chapter III
"Baptized"

If we are going to truly abide in the Vine we need to follow Jesus example. How ridiculous it would be to take instruction on river-boarding and never get in the water or simply wade in to ankle deep. The same is true of our living an abiding life with our Lord and Saviour, Jesus Christ in the river of life at face level. Our Lord expects us to follow Him completely as daily we become more like Him. When James and John wanted to have special places of honor in Jesus Kingdom, He said to them in Matthew 20:22-23, ".......Ye know not what ye ask. Are ye able to drink of the cup that I shall drink of and to be baptized with the baptism that I am baptized with? They say unto Him, we are able. And He saith unto them, ye shall drink indeed of My cup, and be baptized with the baptism that I am baptized with: but to sit on My right hand and on My left, is not mine to give, but it shall be given to them for whom it is prepared of My Father." As you shall see as we continue on into this chapter, Jesus was not talking of following Him in the waters of baptism but was speaking of all the aspects of baptism.

The word baptizmo means to make overwhelmed, fully wet, saturated. In other words every cell in our being is permeated, filled to the point of being overwhelmed or unable to contain any more. There are many baptisms or actually aspects of baptism for all of them involve our being saturated with the presence of the living God. So as we look at each in detail remember that to abide means entering into a relationship and staying there. To be baptized in the sense that Jesus desires requires that we live a life in the river of life at face level with the source of life,[Jesus Christ]! The first aspect of baptism is the baptism of repentance. There is actually only one baptism with many aspects and the following scriptures I list here deal with each aspect. I hope the following diagram along with the scriptures will serve to make it clear. When the word of God speaks of baptism it is speaking of only one baptism which is made up to the following aspects: listed here and repeated below.

1) Christ's love - it is because of His love that we come to Him
2) Repentance - turn from sin unto God
3) Christ's Death - we are buried with Him
4) Christ's Suffering - We identify with and suffer with
5) Into Christ and The Body of Christ - we are one
6) Christ's Resurrection - we are raised with Him [new life]
7) Water Baptism - An outward sign of a change within
8) Baptism of the Holy Spirit - purged and empowered for ministry
9) Baptism of Fire - Come forth as pure gold.

Baptism requires that we accept God's free gift of love through our Lord's atoning work upon the cross. On acceptance of that we turn from sin unto God which requires us to believe - Romans 10:9-10 which = Salvation and Baptism - Mark 16:16 and Ephesians 4:4-6 which places us into Christ and His body - I Corinthians 12:13. At that point we become partakers of His death, His suffering His eternal love and His resurrection. - Galatians 3:26-27, Galatians 2:20 and Romans 6:3-11.

When we enter the waters of baptism we are not being saved we are already saved and simply showing the world with an outward sign what has taken place within and being obedient to follow Jesus in all things. Salvation is a free gift not of works. The aspect of the Baptism of the Holy Spirit and Fire cleanses purges and empowers you for living life in the river of life at face level.

ONE BAPTISM WITH MANY ASPECTS
(Romans 6:3-11, Ephesians 4:4-6, Mark 16:15-18, Romans 10:9-10, I Corinthians 12:13, Galatians 3:26-27, Galatians 2:20)

- ● Christ's Love
- ● Repentance
- ● Christ's Death
- ● Christ's Suffering
- ● Fire
- ● Into Christ & The Body of Christ
- ● Water Baptism
- ● Christ's Resurrection
- ● Baptism of the Holy Spirit

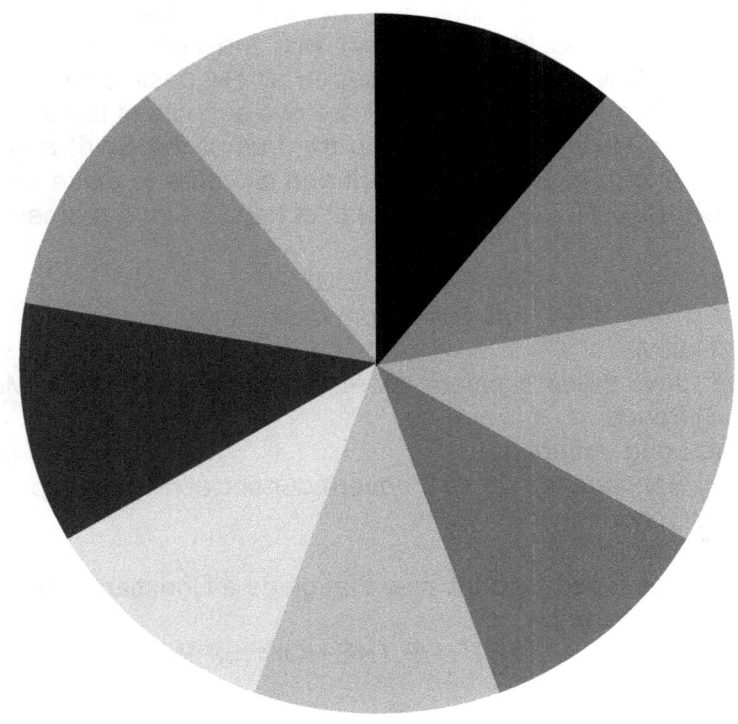

Remember that the word Baptism means to be completely filled or saturated in some way where there is no room for anything else. If you take a log and fill every cell in that log with water it will no longer float in the water but will be submerged becoming one with the water. In the same way when we are baptized into the one baptism we become saturated with all that entails and become one with the Lord and the body of Christ. We identify with Christ and the Holy Spirit and become one with the entire Godhead and the body of Christ As we do we receive all that the Father provides, all that Christ did and all that the Holy Spirit works in and through our lives as together we are being made into the likeness of the Lord and become heirs and joint heirs with Christ Jesus. Since baptism encompasses many aspects and all are vital to our becoming one with the Lord we need to understand the importance of fully involving ourselves in every aspect of baptism. In the same way that the Lord told the disciples that they would be baptized with the Holy Spirit we too must fully immerse ourselves in all He desires to work in and through our lives. Their are two aspects of the baptism of the Holy Spirit the one is the fruit of the Spirit and the other is the Gifts of the Spirit and all come to make us like Christ. Let's look at this aspect of baptism for a moment:

FRUIT OF THE SPIRIT
all come from God

1) Love
2) Joy - these 3 govern our attitudes toward God and Man
3) Peace
4) Long-suffering
5) Gentleness - these 3 govern our social relationships
6) Goodness
7) Faith
8) Meekness - 3 principles that guide a Christian's conduct
9) Temperance

GIFTS OF THE HOLY SPIRIT

(Given as needed by the Spirit that the Spirit filled believer would profit with all and that God's work would move in power)

1) A word of wisdom
2) A word of Knowledge - the revelation gifts
3) Discerning of spirits
4) Faith
5) The gifts of healings - the action gifts
6) Working of miracles
7) Prophecy
8) Divers kinds of tongues -the spoken gifts
9) Interpretation of tongues

Since the Holy Spirit is the Paraclete or the one called along side to be with us and in us forever to guide us into all truth we need to realize that the baptism of the Holy Spirit is not a one time event but is instead an ongoing event as God is working in us to make us like Jesus.

At salvation the Holy Spirit comes within the believer along with Christ as you are baptized into the body of Christ. At that moment you become the temple of the Holy Spirit and He brings with Him the Fruit of the Spirit. Fruit must grow and mature which require time and proper nourishment from the Vine. The gifts are also present, but at the time of what is referred to as the baptism of the Holy Spirit or the second work of grace, we receive the gifts along with the purifying fire as we are filled to overflowing with all that the Holy Spirit wants to work in and through our lives. In order for this to happen we must earnestly seek the gifts as we yield to the Giver [the Holy Spirit]. Don't ever ask the question, "How can I get more of the Holy Spirit?" He is present in His fulness. The question you must ask is, "How can the Holy Spirit have more of me?"

There are nine fruit and nine gifts, and while there are other gifts that come from God the Father, and Christ the

Son, these that come with the Holy Spirit come to fill and mature us, purify us and empower us to minister unto God and for God, in serving man, and witnessing of Jesus Christ to all the World. It is only through the balanced walk in the Spirit that we can overcome the works of the flesh. The nine fruit must mature in your life and the nine gifts must be active in your life to be completely balanced and productive. Don't let man tell you you can't have it all. When it comes to God's provision, He meant it all for YOU! Don't sell yourself short. GOD IS GREAT AND GOD IS AWESOME!!!!!!!

THE FLESH CAN RAISE IT'S UGLY HEAD AT ANY TIME.
The Works of the flesh are these: Adultery, Fornication, Uncleanness, Lasciviousness, [unbridled lust or indecency] Variance [contention], Emulations [jealousies], Wrath, Strife [selfish ambition], Seditions [dissensions], Heresies [self-willed opinions in opposition to the truth], Envying, Murders, Drunkenness, Revelings.

Through the baptism of the Holy Spirit we give ourselves over to God allowing the Holy Spirit to do a work of purifying our lives, filling us to overflowing with His power and person as He gives us gifts to effectively work the works of God. He also brings with Him the fire which purifies and ignites us to zealously witness of the Good News of Jesus Christ. Neither Water Baptism nor the Baptism of the Holy Spirit saves you.

Salvation comes by faith and trust in the completed work upon the cross through the shed blood of our Lord and Saviour Jesus Christ. Both water baptism and Holy Spirit baptism are commanded by our Lord to follow Him in all things and both follow [BAPTISM INTO CHRIST AND THE ONE BODY]. You can be baptized into water or the Spirit in either order. Either can occur first but they both follow belief which through acceptance of what Christ did on the cross brings salvation and enters you into the ONE BAPTISM!.

Because there has been so much misunderstanding on Baptism that has caused much division in the Body of Christ you will find me repeating many times for emphasis the different aspects of the **one baptism** as does the word of God. And as we do I pray that you will understand the vital importance of being baptized in every sense of the word. For as we do we draw into a deeper abiding relationship with our Lord Jesus Christ. Our abiding relationship is a complete merging of lives into Christ Himself where we eventually not only become like Him but we become one with Him. again let me say that when it comes to the aspect of water baptism it does not save us but it is an outward sign of the inward change and we do it in obedience to Jesus command to follow Him in all things. He said that it behoved Him to go into the waters of baptism to fulfill all righteousness. Jesus didn't need to be baptized for repentance or to wash away His sin for He was without sin. He expects us to follow His example and enter the waters of baptism. The water baptism doesn't literally wash away our sins, that took place the moment you accepted Jesus Christ as your personal Saviour. It was then that you were made clean, saved by the power of God through the death and resurrection of Jesus Christ and the word of your testimony. Water baptism is a sign to all that see that your life is now in Him. Romans 5:8-11 says, "But God commendeth His love toward us, in that, while we were yet sinners, Christ died for us. Much more then, being now justified by His blood we shall be saved from wrath through Him. For if when we were enemies, we were reconciled to God by the death of His Son, much more, being reconciled, we shall be saved by His life. And not only so, but we also joy in God through our Lord Jesus Christ, by whom we have now received the atonement." And in Romans 10:9-10 it says, "That if thou shalt confess with thy mouth the Lord Jesus, and shalt believe in thine heart that God hath raised Him from the dead, thou shalt be saved." The moment you received salvation through Jesus Christ you were baptized into Christ and entered a face level relationship with eternal life. What is described in Romans 6:3-11 is what took place upon your confession of Christ as Lord and Saviour. As you enter the water of baptism you are symbolically showing the world the change that has taken place in your life. It is that simple. "Know ye not, that as many of us as were baptized into Jesus Christ were baptized into His death? Therefore we are buried with Him, by baptism into death that like as Christ was raised up from the dead by the glory of the Father, even so we also should walk in newness of life. For if we have been planted together in the likeness of His resurrection: Knowing this that our old man is crucified with Him, that the body of sin might be destroyed, that henceforth we should not serve sin. For he that is dead is freed from sin. Now if we be dead with Christ we believe that we shall also live with Him: Knowing that Christ being raised from the dead dieth no more; death hath no more dominion over Him. For in that He died, He died unto sin once: but in that He liveth He liveth unto God. Likewise reckon ye also yourselves to be dead indeed unto sin but alive unto God through Jesus Christ our Lord."

As we abide in Christ we must fully identify with His death and suffering. Remember baptism means to be overwhelmed, completely saturated or filled to capacity. Ephesians 4:5 tells us, "ONE LORD, ONE FAITH, ONE BAPTISM." The entire aspects of baptism involve our saturated relationship with Jesus Christ. The arguments that the one baptism is water or that the one baptism is in the Spirit are hollow for the truth is to be fully baptized or saturated require that we follow our Lord completely. Both as well as all the other aspects of baptism are part of the abiding life we are to have at face level with Christ. All are important aspects of being baptized into one body and into Christ. I Corinthians 12:13 says, "For by one Spirit are we all baptized into one body, whether we be Jews or Gentiles, whether we be bond or free; and have been all made to drink into one Spirit." And Galatians 3:26-28 says, "For ye are all the children of God by faith in Christ Jesus. For as many of you as have been baptized into Christ have put on Christ. There is neither Jew nor Greek, there is neither bond nor free, there is neither male nor female: for ye are all one in Christ Jesus." When God's word speaks of one baptism it is speaking of the unified aspect of the body being one with Christ. It was His death that removed the wall separating us, both from God and from one another. The more you understand the abiding relationship the greater becomes your understanding of the Christian Walk and life in the river of life.

When Peter was sent to the house of Cornelius and preached the good news of Jesus Christ those Gentiles who heard the word were filled, saturated or baptized with the Holy Spirit as the 120 in the upper room were on the day of Pentecost. Acts 1o:44-48 reads, "While Peter yet spake these words the Holy Ghost fell on them which heard the word. And they of the circumcision which believed, were astonished, as many as came with Peter, because that on the Gentiles also was poured out the gift of the Holy Ghost. For they heard them speak with tongues, and magnify God. Then answered Peter, can any man forbid water, that these should not be baptized, which have received the Holy Ghost as well as we? and He commanded them to be baptized in the name of the Lord. Then prayed they him to tarry certain days." In Acts 1:5 Jesus had spoken to His followers these words, "For John truly baptized with water but ye shall be baptized with the Holy Ghost not many days hence." On the day of Pentecost as they became unified and in one accord we know that, that is exactly what took place. Now we see the Gentiles being baptized as they receive Christ and Peter's obedience in baptizing them in water as a sign of the inward change. To be fully baptized into Christ requires that the established relationship with the Spirit of God results in our living and walking in the Spirit and functioning in the gifts and the fruit of the Spirit.

In I Corinthians 12:4-13 Paul lays out the gifts of the Holy Spirit made available to he believer as each is baptized into Christ and His body. Paul also points out the importance of all the gifts of the Spirit, the need for the gifts, and the fact that they are given by the Holy Spirit when and as they are needed. "Now there are diversities of gifts but the same Spirit. And there are differences of administration,but the same Lord. And there are diversities of operations but it is the same God which worketh all in all. But the manifestation of the Spirit is given every man to profit withal. For to one is given by the Spirit the word of wisdom: to another the word of knowledge by the same Spirit: To another faith by the same Spirit; to another the gifts of healing by the same Spirit: To another the working of miracles; to another prophecy; to another divers kinds of tongues; to another the interpretation of tongues: But all these worketh that one and the selfsame Spirit, dividing to every man severally as He will. For the body is one, and hath many members, and all the members of that one body, being many, are one body; so also is Christ. For by one Spirit are we all baptized into one body, whether we be Jews or Gentiles, whether we be bond or free; and have been all made to drink into one Spirit."

Notice that there are different ways the gifts are administered, different or diverse ways they operate and different gifts but **ONE GOD, ONE LORD AND ONE SPIRIT** all operating as one and God works all the gifts in all the believers. In other words all the gifts are available to every believer when the gifts are needed. Notice also that the manifestation or function or exhibition of the gifts of the Spirit is given to every man to profit with every gift.

Don't ever say my gift is such and such. Now there are office gifts and character gifts which are many but we are simply speaking here of the nine gifts of the Spirit which are given out for the purpose of empowering the believer for service. These nine gifts are available for each of you when they are needed and the Holy Spirit will not withhold them from those who are abiding in Christ and following Him Faithfully at face level in the river of life.

Now if you are truly baptized into Christ there is another side of what is provided by the Holy Spirit and that is the Fruit of the Spirit. Now while the gifts of the Spirit are given to empower us the fruit of the Spirit are provided to purify our lives and enable us to interact with all people while being a true example to the world of a godly Christian. Just as there are nine gifts of the Spirit there are also nine fruit of the Spirit. Each is meant to replace negative fruit of the flesh and with both the gifts and fruit of the Spirit in operation we are meant to walk in a productive, fruitful way with a balanced walk, living at face level with our Lord, empowered for service, serving God and touching man with the love of the Lord.

We find the fruit of the Spirit in Galatians 5:22-23 and the fruit of the flesh or works of the flesh which I listed earlier in Galatians 5:19-21. Let's look at the entire section together beginning at Galatians 5:16 through verse 25 and as we do you will notice that there are many more works of the flesh listed than fruit of the Spirit and the list could go on and on and on.

Man is born with a sin nature because of the fall and therefore has a propensity to sin but through salvation and the infilling of the Holy Spirit God has provided for all of His children the power and means to overcome sin and to be free from the work of the flesh. As we grow in grace and abide in the Vine, yield our will to His leading, and trust and follow Christ as we journey through this life we will know and understand victory. We will also become fruitful and bring glory to our Heavenly Father.

Galatians 5:16-25 reads as follows, "This I say then, Walk in the Spirit and ye shall not fulfill the lust of the flesh. For the flesh lusteth against the Spirit, and the Spirit against the flesh and these are contrary the one to the other: so that ye cannot do the things that ye would. But if ye be led of the Spirit, ye are not under the law. Now the works of the flesh are manifest which are these; Adultery, fornication, uncleanness, lasciviousness, idolatry, witchcraft, hatred, variance, emulations, wrath, strife, seditions, heresies, envyings, murders, drunkenness, revellings and such like of the which I tell you before, as I have also told you in time past, that they which do such things shall not inherit the Kingdom of God. But the fruit of the Spirit is love, joy, peace, longsuffering, gentleness, goodness, faith, meekness, temperance: against such there is no law. And they that are Christ's have crucified the flesh with the affections and lusts. If we live in the Spirit, let us also walk in the Spirit."

When you physically run white water you can find yourself tempted to take a different route than your guide, but you need to understand that your guide knows the river and understands the dangers that lurk beneath the surface. You might be tempted to go a different way because of the challenge or excitement it brings or perhaps because it looks like the easy way. Believe me it is much better to follow the leading and advice of those who have gone before.

As we travel through the river of life we also need to be aware of the hidden dangers that lie beneath the surface, and flee from any temptation that could cause us to sin. Just remember that as long as you are abiding in Christ and have your eyes fixed upon Him, you will always see the way of escape. Don't ever be fooled into thinking that you can just avoid the pitfalls at any time. Redirect your course before it is too late. Our Lord promises that He will make a way of escape and never allow you to be tempted beyond what you can endure but He will not just remove the test or temptation and without an abiding Spirit filled relationship you can never overcome all you face in your own strength.

Let's take a few minutes to look at the meanings of the works of the flesh and as we do remember these two things. First remember that Jesus ,as a man was tempted in every way that you and I are tempted, but without sin. He gave in to NO temptation! Second, we need to remember that the flesh lusteth against the Spirit, or desires the things that are contrary to the Spirit and the Spirit desires those things that are contrary to the fleshly desires. It is only as we are led of the Spirit that we can overcome the natural desires of the flesh.

Listed below are the meanings of the works of the flesh given by Paul:

1. Adultery - an illicit relationship, either sexual or spiritual outside of marriage or covenant relationship.
2. Fornication - to indulge in unlawful lust of either sex or practice idolatry, which is figurative harlotry.
3. Uncleanness - both physical and moral impurity.
4. Lasciviousness - wantonness or one who is filthy in actions.
5. Idolatry - image worship or service, contrary to true worship of God.
6. Witchcraft - Greek work Pharmakia, magic, drug use or sorcery.
7. Hatred - hostility or enmity toward another.
8. Variance - wrangling, contention, debate {a spirit of argumentation}.

9. Emulations - unfavorable jealousy or indignation or malice.
10. Wrath - fierce indignation or enraged passion.
11. Strife - to provoke, cause faction or contention.
12. Seditions - dissension, division and disunion.
13. Heresies - falsehood, not unified with the truth.
14. Envyings - jealousy or ill-will toward another.
15. Murders - those who slay or slaughter others.
16. Drunkenness - intoxication by means of alcohol or drugs.
17. Revellings - letting loose, carousing or rioting.

Since all sexual sin involving a child of God is a breaking of the covenant relationship you have with the Lord you can understand how this becomes idolatry. This also explains why David after His sin with Bathsheba said to the Lord in Psalm 51:4, "Against Thee, and Thee only, have I sinned, and done this evil in Thy sight that Thou mightest be justified when thou speakest and be clear when Thou judgest." Now look at I Corinthians 6:12-20, "All things are lawful unto me but all things are not expedient: All things are lawful for me, but I will not be brought under the power of any. Meats for the belly and the belly for meats: but God shall destroy both it and them. Now the body is not for fornication, but for the Lord and the Lord for the body. And God hath both raised up the Lord, and will also raise up us by His own power. Know ye not that your bodies are the members of Christ? shall I then take the members of Christ and make them the members of a harlot? God forbid. What? know ye not that he which is joined to an Harlot is one body? for two saith He shall be one flesh. But he that is joined unto the Lord is one spirit. Flee fornication. Every sin that a man doeth is without the body; but he that commiteth fornication sinneth against his own body. What? know ye not that your body is the temple of the Holy Ghost which is in you, which ye have of God, and ye are not your own? For ye are bought with a price: therefore glorify God in your body and in your spirit, which are God's."

The Greek word Porneia is translated harlotry, including adultery, fornication and idolatry. From the meaning of the word any unlawful lust [of either sex] makes the perpetrator, a harlot, joined to a harlot. Any breaking of covenant relationship is a serious offense against the Lord with whom you are spiritually joined and this includes any thoughts or viewing of porn.

Because of the extreme dangers we face in this life God has provided for us everything we need to safely navigate through the rapids avoiding the underlying dangers. He has provided His Holy Spirit to dwell within and tells us that we are the temple of the Holy Spirit. Where the Spirit of God is , no evil can dwell, and where the Spirit of God is there is liberty. We are truly free from the bondage of sin. The presence of the Spirit not only equips us for the battles and dangers we face but He also provides us with the graces to smoothy get through all the tests and trials we will encounter.

If we face these trials in the flesh we will most often give in to the works of the flesh and be given over to or driven by our desires or the natural man. The works of the flesh could be placed into a single category [Selfishness]. Whether they are sins of a sexual nature, false religion or idolatrous nature, sins of anger or excess or rebellion all are sins that damage the intimacy established within a covenant relationship and can not only greatly hurt your relationship with those closest to us and our brothers and sisters in the Lord but can render us defenseless and ineffective in the battles we face and destroy the abiding relationship and render us fruitless.

if we live and walk in the Spirit we will not be given over to the deeds of the flesh, for where the fruit of the Spirit are abundantly evident and mature, the works of the flesh have no power over the individual. also when we are abiding in an intimate relationship the Holy Spirit will equip us to meet every need and overcome every obstacle.

Let's look now at the fruit of the Spirit provided for us to give us the victorious and joyful life God intends for us to have. Jesus said in John 10:10, "The thief cometh not but for to steal, and to kill and to destroy: I have come that they might have life and that they might have it more abundantly." The works of the flesh are the plan of the thief meant to destroy. The fruit of the Spirit is the plan of the Lord meant to give abundant life.

1. Love - The Greek word [agape] is a completely unselfish and benevolent love which gives out love or charity whether any love is returned.
2. Joy - The Greek word here is [chara] which comes from the root chairo - to be calmly happy or well off. the full meaning adding cheerfulness and being exceedingly glad, calm and full of joy.
3. Peace - The word [eirene] - implying prosperity, one, peace, quietness, and rest and set at one again.
4. Longsuffering - [meekesthumia] the Greek word translated longsuffering means forbearance, fortitude and patience.
5. Gentleness - The Greek word [cherstates] includes excellence in character or demeanor and kindness.
6. Goodness - The Greek word [agathosune] also means virtue or beneficence.
7. Faith - The Greek word translated faith here is [pistis] and means persuasion or conviction of the truthfulness of God and assurance of and reliance upon Christ for salvation and faithfulness.
8. Meekness - [proates] add humility. a humble confidence which displays a gentle character.
9. Temperance - [egkrateia] also self control and continence.

Verse 24 of Galatians 5 tells us that if we are Christ's we have crucified the flesh with the affections and lusts. That being the case we should not allow the dead to rise its ugly head. We should not give in to the works of the flesh. In verse 25 Paul says, since we live in the Spirit we should walk in the Spirit. Doing that will solidify our abiding relationship with Christ. In order for that to happen we must exhibit the mature fruit of the Spirit. In the natural none of us are capable of loving the way God does but the Spirit provides that unselfish total giving, no strings attached agape love. Let it be seen in all you do. The fruit of joy we receive is fulness of joy, unspeakable and full of glory which allows us to display a calmness and be happy and cheerful no matter what obstacles we face. The peace we receive is a peace that brings quietness and spiritual prosperity as we enter into the promised rest our Lord promised and live in the abundance of spiritual prosperity and life.

Now if you can display maturity in Love, Joy and Peace you are off to a great start but there are still six more. To truly display longsuffering goes against the grain of every fiber in the natural man. To forbear in difficult or dangerous places or show patience in uncomfortable situations takes a supernatural gift that is difficult to hang onto but this is exactly what is necessary to fully abide in the Vine. And then there is the fruit of gentleness which requires an excellence in character and behavior and kindness. In order to be honest, truthful and kind all at once can be a very touchy balancing act that requires that you always seek and rely upon the leading of the Holy Spirit. And then what about goodness? Jesus, himself said, "Why call ye Me good. There is none good but God." Of course Jesus is God and He wasn't denying that. He was actually drawing attention to that very fact and we need to realize that it is only by the righteousness of God and His goodness that goodness can exist in our lives. Without Christ and the indwelling of the Holy Spirit virtue is not ours. We are only virtuous and beneficent as the goodness of God is revealed through our words and deeds.

The last four reveal just how strong and intimate is our relationship with our Lord. To walk in faith requires our total trust in God and His Word; reliance on our salvation provided by Christ, and our being faithful with all He has entrusted to us and that includes being faithful to His word and our service unto Him. Meekness brings out in us an aspect of the word that many misunderstand. Meekness is not weakness but instead gentle humility under pressure. Being meek is not relying on your own strength but instead knowing who you are and what your purpose is in Christ and boldly fulfilling that purpose knowing that without Him you can do nothing but through Christ you can do all things. And finally the fruit of temperance. This is being under self control and that can only happen as we yield to the leading of the Spirit and understand the importance of our place as those who inherit all things. As priests and kings or princes in God's kingdom we are not to be given to wine or strong drink and if our desire is to be led of the Spirit and abide in the Vine then we need to understand and adhere to the principle laid out in Ephesians 5:15-21 where Paul clearly states the will of God for all of us who call Him Lord and Saviour. "See then that ye walk circumspectly, not as fools, but as wise. Redeeming the time, because the days are evil. Wherefore be ye not unwise, but understanding what the will of the Lord is. and be not drunk with wine , wherein is excess but be filled with the Spirit; Speaking to yourselves in psalms and hymns and spiritual songs, singing and making melody in your heart to the Lord: Giving thanks always for all things unto God and the Father in the name of our Lord Jesus Christ; Submitting yourselves one to another in the fear of God."

It is God's will, His purpose, that we be filled with the Spirit. If we are we will be so full of joy that we will live a life of praise and worship and be thankful for everything that comes our way knowing that He is in control and through Him we can face every obstacle and no matter how bad it seems if we have God and are the called according to His purpose in the end He will bring good from it. And from this position we can willingly submit to one another and grow in relationships as we do so in the awesome reverential fear of God. Each and every day in each and every way it is God's purpose that we be molded into the likeness and image of Christ. Oh to be more like Him.

In Matthew 20:22-23 the cup Jesus was referring to was the cup and baptism of suffering and that aspect of baptism we quickly want to avoid but if we are to rule and reign with Him we must truly be willing to suffer with Him and fully identify with all He has undergone and follow Him in every way in the river of life. Paul said he wanted one thing and one thing only and that was to know and understand fully the suffering and death and resurrection of Christ and all He preached revolved around the cross of Christ.

In Philippians 3:7-14 Paul states, "But what things were gain for me those I counted loss for Christ. Yea doubtless, and I count all things but loss for the excellency of the knowledge of Christ Jesus my Lord for when I have suffered the loss of all things, and do count them but dung, that I may win Christ, and be found in Him, not having mine own righteousness, which is of the law but that which is through the faith of Christ, the righteousness which is of God by faith; That I may know Him, and the power of His resurrection and the fellowship of His sufferings, being made conformable unto His death; If by any means I might attain unto the resurrection of the dead. Not as though I had already attained, either were already perfect, but I follow after, if that I may apprehend that for which also I am apprehended of Christ Jesus. Brethren, I count not myself to have apprehended; but this one thing I do, forgetting those things which are behind, and reaching forth unto those things which are before, I press toward the mark for the prize of the high calling of God in Christ Jesus."

Paul wished to be fully immersed in the sufferings of our Lord and conformable unto His death so that he might attain unto the resurrection of the dead. This is what it means to be fully baptized into Christ as His body and one with Him!

Chapter IV
"TOSSED TO AND FRO "

If you have ever ridden a bull or a bronco or been tossed from a river board in white water then you understand what it means to be tossed to and fro. Each and everyone of us as we travel the river of life have known times, or you will, when it seems like everything is coming at you from every direction and just when you think you finally have your sea legs you get blindsided again. So what do we do under such conditions? It is times like that, that you fix your attention on a focal point you can trust in front of you and relax. Oh yeh you say, relax, sure thing, my head is spinning around and everything is upside down and I don't know which way is up. And focus, on what? I can't see the same direction for more than a split second.

I completely understand! The focal point is focussing on what you have learned and what you know is true and what you can trust in. When you do that riding a bull for 8 seconds is not so bad and reconnoitering and connecting with your board and again smoothly maneuvering through the rapids is a thrill and a joy. More importantly as your focal point in life is your relationship and trust in the Lord, the things that come crashing down upon you and seem to be tossing you to and fro become that 8 second ride.

In the book of James; in the first chapter James talks about those things that come to test us and tempt us and knock us off course and He says it is for our growth and to turn us to our focal point but he also says if we waver in our focus we are double minded and like a wave of the sea driven with the wind and tossed. If we are tossed to and fro by our failure to trust and focus there will be no help.

Look at James 1:1-7, "James a servant of God and the Lord Jesus Christ, to the twelve tribes which are scattered abroad, greetings. My brethren, count it all joy when ye fall into divers temptations; Knowing this, that the trying of your faith worketh patience. But let patience have her perfect work, that ye may be perfect and entire, wanting nothing. If any of you lack wisdom, let him ask of God, that giveth to all men liberally, and upbraideth not; and it shall be given him. But let him ask in faith, nothing wavering. For he that wavereth is like a wave of the sea driven with the wind and tossed. For let not that man think that he shall receive anything of the Lord; A double minded man is unstable in all his ways."

If the river you run is always smooth you will never learn to ride the rapids or grow in your ability as a river-boarder. You will never learn to focus on your teacher or the things you are being taught and when you do face a rapid that is violent or an obstacle too difficult to transverse you will find yourself tossed to and fro and in trouble beyond what you can handle and instead of relying on what you know you should do you will waver in your decision and never find a stable course. As we travel the river of life the same thing is true. It will not always be smooth sailing.

When you begin to face bigger and stronger rapids to get through in the river on a river-board you experience the thrill of accomplishment and victory and the joy that accompanies it. Now we are told in the book of James that we are to count it all joy when we fall into divers temptations. We might add to this the same attitude of a river-boarder. There is always the thrill of knowing you are facing something bigger than you but you can conquer it. God allows the tests, trials and temptations to come our way and gives us the ability and help to get through each and ever one.

All the tests we face are meant to add virtue to our lives not destroy us. The word says that it is the trying or testing of our faith that brings patience. Step back and take a good hard look at what James is saying. When we face obstacles and find things coming against us it is not the natural man that is being tested [IT IS OUR FAITH]. Let me repeat myself just in case you missed it the first time. WHEN TEMPTATIONS OR TESTS OR DIFFICULTIES COME OUR WAY IT IS NOT THE NATURAL MAN BEING TESTED, IT IS OUR FAITH! Are you going to trust the Lord to see you through? Are you going to rely on what you know is true in God's word or will you give way to reacting in the natural and become impatient and look elsewhere for your answer or deal with each test in the natural and in your own way instead of God's way? Remember we are to count it all joy. The situations you face may seem hopeless so get excited. You are about to learn a lesson in patience and perseverance. God's word says that you will never be tempted beyond what you can endure so look for the escape route God is preparing and set your focus upon the Lord. If you are abiding in Him and His word in you just know the answer is not off in the far distance somewhere. It is within; firmly entrenched in your relationship with Jesus.

Well, now that we know what it is that is being tested as we feel bombarded with each attack that comes our way let's learn to allow the trying of our faith to work patience for James 1:4 says, "but let patience have her perfect work, that ye may be perfect and entire, wanting nothing." Whatever you do don't pass off that statement lightly for there is a lot of heavy truth wrapped up in that statement. First of all the word [hupomone] which is translated patience means cheerful or hopeful endurance. When we are waiting for answers or a change or door of escape are we cheerful and hopefully enduring the problems we face? When we get to the point where we realize that it is our faith, [our abiding relationship that is being tested], it is much easier for us to trust and wait cheerfully and hopefully for the promised answer and place it all in the Lord's hands. the statement says that we are to let patience, [cheerful hopeful endurance], have her perfect work. Perfect here is the word [teleios] meaning complete. As you wait cheerfully and hopefully while enduring, that patience will bring about in you the complete work God desires, making you perfect. The Greek word [teleios] in the application here takes on the meaning of complete in moral character and entire [holokleros] meaning complete in every part, perfectly sound in body; wanting nothing. Now just how does patience accomplish so much?

Romans 5:1-5 says, "Therefore being justified by faith we have peace with God through our Lord Jesus Christ: By whom also we have access by faith into this grace wherein we stand and rejoice in hope of the glory of God. And not only so but we glory in tribulations also knowing that tribulation worketh patience; and patience experience; and experience, hope: And hope maketh not ashamed: because the love of God is shed abroad in our hearts by the Holy Ghost which is given unto us." James says count it all joy when we face tests and trials and Paul says, we glory in our tribulations. Now remember James says it is our faith that is being tested. Paul says we are justified by faith and have access into the grace of God through faith and it is in that which we stand rejoicing in the hope of the glory of God and also glory in tribulation because of what it brings. If we have a deep abiding relationship with our Lord, that relationship is established and founded upon our faith in what He has done for us. James says that patience brings us completeness where we lack nothing; and Paul lets us know patience brings experience, and that in turn brings hope and our hope makes us such that we are not ashamed. The word for experience is [dokime] meaning trustiness or more plainly trust through trials. Now the word for hope is [elpis] which means to anticipate with pleasure, confident expectation or faith.   So as you understand that it is your faith that is being tested and through our rejoicing and glorying in our trials and enduring with cheerfulness we are made complete and brought to wholeness through our trust in God to see us through, and our faith is strengthened so we are not ashamed. The word Paul uses here for ashamed is [Kataischuno] which means disgraced, confounded or dishonored. We will not fail the test. The type of patience God provides through a strong faith brings victory. But back to the question. How does this occur? Paul says, "...because the love of God is shed abroad in our hearts by the Holy Ghost which is given unto us." It is as we abide in the Vine, focus on Christ and the truth of His word and live and walk in the Spirit that we live in victory and when things come to cause us to be tossed we remain steadfast.

In II Peter 1:2-10 Peter elaborates on the completeness we receive and what it does for us. It appears that Peter, James and Paul learned from the trials and temptations they faced and from their failures, the purpose for God allowing the obstacles we face in the river of life and the meaning of trust and patient endurance and not wavering but standing in faith. Let's look at II Peter 1;2-10. "Grace and peace be multiplied unto you through the knowledge of God and of Jesus our Lord. According as His divine power hath given unto us all things that pertain unto life and godliness through the knowledge of Him that hath called us to glory and virtue; Whereby are given unto us exceeding great and precious promises that by these ye might be partakers of the divine nature, having escaped the corruption that is in the world through lust. And beside this giving all diligence, add to your faith virtue; and to virtue knowledge; and to knowledge temperance; and to temperance patience; and to patience godliness; and to godliness brotherly kindness; and to brotherly kindness charity. For if these be in you and abound, they make you that ye shall neither be barren nor unfruitful in the knowledge of our Lord Jesus Christ. But he that lacketh these things is blind, and cannot see afar off, and hath forgotten that he was purged from his old sins. Wherefore the rather, brethren, give diligence to make your calling and election sure: for if ye do these things, ye shall never fall:"

Peter lists the things in the way of virtues that we receive by faith and how one is added upon another. Our faith would be lacking if it failed to bring us to maturity. However, along with our faith are the fruit of the Spirit which come as we are baptized into Christ and receive the presence of the Holy Spirit as we saw in our study of the one baptism. As we grow and produce fruit and no longer give in to the works of the flesh we become mature. Notice that the completeness we achieve is godliness, brotherly kindness and agape love, so patience which comes through tribulation should be met with joy for it makes us fruitful lacking nothing.

If we are unsure of what we are to do about the tests or trials or problems we face and therefore lack wisdom we need to ask God and He will give us that which we need. Only when we ask we must ask in faith believing and doubt not. We cannot waver in our faith or we will find ourselves tossed to and fro and we won't get the answer, direction or help we need, for as James tells us from God's word, "A double minded man is unstable in all his ways." It is up to each of us. We can make our focal point the abiding life in Jesus Christ and totally trust in Him and the word of God and live in the Spirit and joyfully go through every test learning patience and growing in the knowledge of Jesus Christ as we become perfect and entire wanting nothing or we can go our own way and allow doubts to rob us of victory.

Chapter V
"FAITH"

Without faith it is impossible to please God and through faith we can move mountains. We have seen that the trying of our faith brings us into maturity and makes us fruitful but I don't want us to just brush over faith. So let's look at the different aspects of faith and how they affect us and influence our abiding relationship with Christ.

First of all let's look at what constitutes faith! Hebrews 11:1 says, "Now faith is the substance of things hoped for the evidence of things not seen." Now let's break this down.

Faith - [pistis] from this word comes persuasion, credence, conviction of the truthfulness of God; reliance upon Christ for salvation; assurance in the Good News and belief in the truth of God's word.

It is the **Substance** [hupostasis] - a setting under or support

of **Things** [pragma] a deed, an affair or a material object

Hoped [elpizo] to expect to have or trust

for the **Evidence** [elegchos] proof, conviction

of things not **Seen** [blepa] to look at or on, to behold.

Faith is what everything revolves around. It is the solid support or under pinning of the objects or promises of God that we wait expectantly for and trust in. It is the evidence or proof of what we hope for but for now we do not see or behold in the natural but are convinced they are true. So what is our faith? If I give you a piece of land in some place you have never been nor seen, I give you a deed to that land describing it and guaranteeing that you own it . You have never seen it but you hold a piece of paper that tells you all about it and gives you ownership of it. In the natural you are putting your trust and faith in what the deed says. That is how our faith operates. As the deed is evidence of the existence of the land and proof of your ownership, so your faith is evidence of the promises written in God's word and the underpinnings, substance and support of the truth of God's word and the salvation of your soul through your acceptance of the death and resurrection of our Lord Jesus Christ.

The entire eleventh chapter of Hebrews describes what faith does. Verse two tells us the elders received a good report by their faith. Verse three tells us that our understanding of creation comes by our faith in the truth of the word of God that creation took place as recorded in Genesis and what we are told in John 1:1-4, "In the beginning was the Word and the Word was with God and the Word was God. All things were made by Him, and without Him was not anything made that was made. In Him was life and the life was the light of men." Jesus is the Word made flesh and all was created by Him out of nothing. We cannot know this through natural means. We must receive this truth through faith. However, we can see the physical evidence of the truth of creation and the total order of Gods universe.

By faith Abel offered the sacrifice God required and was accepted by God and called righteous even though his brother, who trusted in his own ways and offered sacrifice contrary to God's decree killed him. Enoch's faith in God and His word caused him to receive his own personal rapture. Noah's faith in what God had spoken to him caused him to build an ark by which God saved his family alive and preserved the animals of the world. It also allowed him to preach for over a hundred years to those who mocked and made fun of Noah.

If God has spoken something to you that others don't understand and because of their lack of understanding accuse you of doing your own thing, don't waver. Exercise your faith and trust God. Stand firm no matter how long it takes. When Abraham was called of God to go to a place he had never seen he went not questioning and was a sojourner never having a permanent home for he was looking for a city whose builder and maker was God.

When you have time read Hebrews chapter eleven and you will discover that many of the promises of God men and women of faith put their trust in did not take place in their life times but none the less they were true and are true.

Think how foolish the blood covenant must have sounded to the Jews when Moses told them what they had to do in order for the first born to live through the night and what about facing the red sea trapped on one side by the sea and the other side by the Egyptian army and hearing Moses tell you that you will walk through on dry ground and never see the army again. Moses believed what God said and God did as He said. And what must Joshua have thought when God gave him the strategic plan for the taking of Jericho? We could go on and on and see the results of faith.

Then there are always those who will say yeh but look at all those who were killed and what about the missionaries who leave home feeling called of God to go and then end up dead? Can't you serve God here? Why do you have to go somewhere else? To that let me say this; nothing you do for Christ is a waste. And only those who truly understand the call of God will ever really be able to comprehend the reasons why God has protected some and allowed others to die in His service, but look closely at Hebrews 11:32-40, paying particular attention to verse 40 and realize that the promises of God's word are real and the rewards many and great. Here is how that portion of scripture reads. "And what shall I more say for the time would fail me to tell of Gideon, and of Barak, and of Samson and Jephthah: of David also, and Samuel, and the prophets: Who through faith subdued kingdoms, wrought righteousness, obtained promises, stopped the mouths of Lions. Quenched the violence of fire, escaped the edge of the sword, out of weakness were made strong, waxed valiant in fight, turned to flight the armies of the aliens. Women received their dead raised to life again; and others were tortured, not accepting deliverance, that they might obtain a better resurrection: And others had cruel mockings and scourgings, yea, moreover of bonds and imprisonment: They were stoned, they were sawn asunder, were tempted, were slain with the sword; They wandered about in sheepskins and goatskins; being destitute, afflicted, tormented: (Of whom the world was not worthy;) they wandered in deserts, and in mountains, and in dens and caves of the earth. And these all, having obtained a good report through faith, received not the promise: God having provided some better thing for us, that they without us should not be made perfect."

We could also look at Paul's life and the great accomplishments of faith that took place who in the end faced the guillotine In the end his words were. "I have fought a good fight. I have finished my course. I have kept the faith: Henceforth there is laid up for me a crown of righteousness. Which the Lord, the righteous judge, shall give me at that day and not me only, but unto all them also that love His appearing." II Timothy 4:7-8. Paul hadn't become weak in faith. He knew his time of departure was at hand. He said he had kept the faith. Don't allow even those closest to you whom you love dearly to deter you from the course God puts before you.

Faith is not simply something we see in operation of great men and women of God but in all who trust in Christ and desire to abide in Him. In Matthew 8:5-10 we read this story of a centurion, not a preacher but a professional soldier. "And when Jesus was entered into Capernaum, there came unto Him a centurion, beseeching Him and saying, Lord, my servant lieth at home sick of the Palsy, grievously tormented. And Jesus saith unto him. I will come and heal him. The centurion answered and said, Lord, I am not worthy that thou shouldest come under my roof: but speak the word only, and my servant shall be healed. For I am a man under authority having soldiers under me and I say to this man, Go, and he goeth; and to another, come, and he cometh; and to my servant, Do this, and he doeth it. When Jesus heard it, He marveled, and said to them that followed. Verily I say unto you, I have not found so great faith, no not in Israel."

The faith of the Centurion gave him an understanding of the authority, the Lord had, simply through speaking the word. There is literal power of life and death in what we speak. The More we understand our abiding relationship with the Lord the clearer will become our comprehension of the authority our Lord has entrusted unto us. John 15:7 says, "If ye abide in Me and My words abide in you, ye shall ask what ye will and it shall be done unto you." and Mark 11:23 says, "For I verily say unto you, That whosoever shall say unto this mountain, Be thou removed and be thou cast into the sea: and shall not doubt in his heart, but shall believe that those things which he saith shall come to pass, he shall have whatsoever he saith." The faith by which we move is extremely powerful both positive and negative. And since doubt is faith in reverse we can quickly cancel out God's blessings by allowing doubt to enter in to our thinking or speaking and thereby becoming double minded. As for the Centurion, he was convinced in his heart that Jesus could heal simply by speaking the word and giving the command and he received exactly what he had requested.

In Matthew 9:2-7 we see a second example of how your faith can bring healing to another and in this case we are also told that it brought forgiveness of sins. "And behold they brought to Him a man sick of the palsy, lying on a bed; and Jesus seeing their faith said unto the sick of the palsy; Son be of good cheer: thy sins be forgiven thee. And behold certain of the scribes said within themselves, This man blasphemeth. And Jesus knowing their thoughts said, Wherefore think ye evil in your hearts? For whether is easier, to say, thy sins be forgiven thee; or to say, arise and walk? But that ye may know that the Son of man hath power on earth to forgive sins, [Then saith He to the sick of the palsy], arise, take up thy bed and go unto thine house. And he arose and departed to his house."

Sometimes it seems easy to believe God to heal and meet the needs of others but when it comes to our own needs we lack that faith and put our trust in doctors and at times with no results and we even get worse or in the financial realm we place out trust in banks or government or our jobs and are let down. In physical healing such was the case of the woman we read about in Matthew 9:20-22. "And behold a woman which was diseased with an issue of blood twelve years came behind Him and touched the hem of His garment: For she said within herself, If I may but touch His garment, I shall be whole. But Jesus turned Him about and when He saw her, He said, Daughter, be of good comfort; thy faith hath made thee whole. And the woman was made whole from that hour." The closer you get to Jesus the stronger your faith becomes and the more you operate in faith the greater are the answers. Just remember that you can only receive that which is within the Will of God and the more we understand the word of God and the more of the word that abides within us, the better we understand God's will and the more certain we are that what we ask for is promised within the word.

In Matthew 17:14-21 we see how defeating our unbelief can be and also means of strengthening our faith. "And when they were come to the multitude, there came to Him a certain man, kneeling down to Him, and saying, Lord, have mercy on my son: for he is lunatic, and sore vexed; for ofttimes he falleth into the fire and oft into the water. And I brought him to thy disciples, and they could not cure him. Then Jesus answered and said, O faithless and perverse generation, how long shall I be with you? how long shall I suffer you? bring him hither to me. And Jesus rebuked the devil; and he departed out of him: and the child was cured from that very hour. Then came the disciples to Jesus apart, and said, Why could not we cast him out? And Jesus said unto them; Because of your unbelief: for verily I say unto you, If you have faith as a grain of mustard see, ye shall say unto this mountain, remove hence to yonder place; and it shall remove; and nothing shall be impossible unto you. Howbeit this kind goeth not out but by prayer and fasting."

Prior to this Jesus had given His disciples authority over demons and they had seen that they were subject unto them. But Jesus expressly says they were hindered by their unbelief and follows that by saying that no matter how small their faith that if they exercise that faith through prayer and fasting that they would see miracles. That being true, what is the difference between little faith and the faith the size of a grain of mustard seed? And to start with how do we get faith. Romans 10:11-18 says, "For the scripture saith, whosoever believeth on Him shall not be ashamed. For there is no difference between the Jew and the Greek for the same Lord over all is rich unto all that call upon Him. For whosoever shall call upon the name of the Lord shall be saved. How then shall they call on Him in whom they have not believed? and how shall they believe in Him of Whom they have not heard? and how shall they hear without a preacher? And how shall they preach except they be sent? as it is written, How beautiful are the feet of them that preach the gospel of peace, and bring glad tidings of good things. But they have not all obeyed the gospel. For Esaias saith, Lord who hath believed our report? So then faith cometh by hearing, and hearing by the word of God. But I say, Have they not heard? Yes verily, their sound went into all the earth and their words unto the ends of the World."

So, if faith comes by hearing and the sound of the word has gone into all the earth why is the world so void of faith? And why do so many of those who by faith have believed and called upon the Lord and who are saved, have only little faith and fail to move in faith? The Greek word [akoe] translated hearing means the physical sense of hearing or having given audience to the word preached or reported where the root word to hear [akouo] means to hear and understand. If we were to look at the rest of chapter 10 we would see that Israel had heard and Known the truth but were disobedient and rejected the truth and went their own way. If we look at Matthew 13:11-16 we can get a clearer picture of what happens when we hear but don't hear. Jesus had just spoken to the people in a parable of the sower in verses 3 through 9 when the disciple asked Him why He spoke unto them in parables. In verse nine where He says, hear: it literally means "Who has ears to hear physically and understand let that person Physically hear and understand what is spoken. Verse 14 of Romans 10 literally means, "How then shall they call on Him in whom they have not believed [known and put their trust in]? And how shall they [be committed to put their trust in, and have faith in] believe in Him of whom they have not heard [heard and understood]? and how shall they hear [physically hear and understand] without a preacher?" So now let's go back to the parable of the sower and look at verses 13-16, "Therefore speak I to them in parables; because they seeing see not; and hearing they hear not, neither do they understand. And in them is fulfilled the prophecy of Esaias which saith, By hearing ye shall hear, and shall not understand and seeing ye shall see and not perceive: For this people's heart is waxed gross and their ears are dull of hearing and their eyes they have closed; lest at any time they should see with their eyes and hear with their ears and should understand with their heart and should be converted and I should heal them. But blessed are your eyes, for they see and your ears for they hear."

The more we abide in Christ and His word abides in us, and the longer we travel the river of life the better able we are to see, not just the physical things, but in the Spirit, and see life through God's eyes and the more we understand the word of God. It is one thing to hear the word with our physical ears and it is another thing to understand with our hearts.

In the parable of the sower there were many who physically heard the word but through numerous things were robbed of a true depth of understanding that allowed them, through faith, to become fruitful. In fact, there were many prophets and righteous people who desired to see in the Spirit and fully understand, who saw and heard, but lacked the understanding. So look with me at verses 17-23, "For verily I say unto you. That many prophets and righteous men have desired to see those things which ye see, and have not seen them; and to hear those things which ye hear and have not heard them. Hear ye therefore the parable of the sower. When anyone heareth the word of the kingdom, and understandeth it not, then cometh the wicked one, and catcheth away that which was sown in his heart. This is he which received seed by the way side. But he that receiveth the seed into stony places, the same is he that heareth the word, and anon with joy receiveth it: Yet hath he not root in himself, but dureth for a while; for when tribulation or persecution ariseth because of the word, and by and by he is offended. He also that receiveth seed among the thorns is he that heareth the word: and the care of this world and the deceitfulness of riches, choke the word and he becometh unfruitful. But he that receiveth seed into the good ground is he that heareth the word, and understandeth it: which also beareth fruit, and bringeth forth, some an hundredfold, some sixty, some thirty." Where it says, "...he that receiveth [lambono]- to seize, hold - obtain; seed into good ground is he that heareth [heard and understood] the word, and understandeth [sieniemi] - [to be wise, comprehend and understand] it, which also beareth fruit and bringeth forth, some an hundredfold, some sixth, some thirty."

The reason so few people move in faith is because of the enemy of your soul stealing from you so that you never really reach an understanding of the word that brings strong faith. Also too many people who hear and do understand the word of God fail to have depth of relationship and when persecution and hard tests come, when the rapids get too big and you failed to learn your lessons, it is wipe out. Then, another reason is that too many people don't put the things of God first and are concerned with the things of the world, riches or rewards instead of relationship and come up empty. In order to obtain faith you need to commit to an abiding relationship and hear with understanding and see life through God's eyes.

Now what is the difference between little faith and faith the size of a mustard seed? Look at Matthew 14:22-31. "And straightway Jesus constrained His disciples to get into a ship and go before Him unto the other side, while He sent the multitudes away. And when He had sent the multitudes away, He went up into a mountain apart to pray and when the evening was come, he was there alone. But the ship was now in the midst of the sea tossed with waves for the wind was contrary. And in the fourth watch of the night Jesus went unto them, walking on the sea. and when the disciples saw Him walking on the sea, they were troubled saying, It is a spirit; and they cried out for fear. But straightway Jesus spake unto them, saying, Be of good cheer; It is I be not afraid. And Peter answered Him and said, Lord , if it be Thou, bid me come unto Thee on the water. And He said, come. And when Peter was come down out of the ship, he walked on the water, to go to Jesus. But when he saw the wind boisterous, he was afraid; and beginning to sink, he cried, saying, Lord save me. And immediately Jesus stretched forth His hand, and caught him, and said unto him, O thou of little faith, wherefore didst thou doubt? As long as Peter kept his eyes on the Lord he had functioning faith but when his eyes turned to the circumstances his faith failed and doubt took over.

We also have the story of Jesus asleep in the ship as the disciples were fighting to keep the ship afloat in a great storm. We read this in Mark 4:38-41, "And He was in the hinder part of the ship asleep on a pillow, and they awake Him and say unto Him, Master, carest Thou not that we perish? And He arose, and rebuked the wind, and said unto the sea, Peace! be still. And the wind ceased, and there was a great calm. And He said unto them, Why are ye so fearful? How is it that ye have no faith? And they feared exceedingly, and said one to another, What manner of man is this , that even the wind and the sea obey Him?"

The disciples, like so many Christians today, find themselves in the presence of the Lord and yet are so overcome by the circumstances they find themselves in, instead of trusting and moving in faith they cry out in fear and then when the Lord answers they find it hard to believe and instead of growing in faith and understanding more, they scratch their heads and say how can this be? It appalls me when people look for a natural answer today for why miracles happen instead of believing God. I am grieved and I am sure the Lord is grieved when those who know me and have seen the miracles God has worked in my life come up with their own explanations for what took place. God is the same yesterday, today and forever and is still working miracles and just because there have been times He has not chosen to work a miracle in my life or through my life doesn't discount those He has worked. Remember when we looked at Matthew 17:14-21 Jesus said that if they had faith as a grain of mustard seed they would see miracles. Now bear with me for I firmly believe that Jesus was not simply drawing a comparison with the size of their faith, but instead the quality of their faith. This is not the only time Jesus uses a mustard seed to draw a picture to use as an example to teach a great lesson. In the parable of the mustard seed in Luke 13:18-19 Jesus said, "......unto what is the kingdom of God like? and whereunto shall I resemble it? It is like a grain of mustard seed which a man took, and cast into his garden: and it grew and waxed a great tree and the fowls of the air lodged in the branches of it." A mustard seed is useless unless planted and then it is very productive and useful. In the same way our faith is useless unless used for the intended purpose. I challenge you to put your faith to work and watch it grow and be productive. When Jesus cursed the fig tree His disciples were amazed at how soon it had withered and died and in Matthew 21:21-22, "Jesus answered and said unto them, Verily I say unto you, If ye have faith and doubt not ye shall not only do this which is done to the fig tree, but also if ye say unto this mountain, Be thou removed and be thou cast into the sea it shall be done. and all things whatsoever ye shall ask in prayer, believing ye shall receive." Always remember for faith to work it cannot be coupled with doubt because doubt is faith in reverse. One other thing you must always be aware of is the fact that God will not answer prayer that goes against His Word.

To follow this further look at Mark 11:22-24. "And Jesus answering saith unto them, Have faith in God. For verily I say unto you, That whosoever shall say unto this mountain, Be thou removed, and cast into the sea and shall not doubt in his heart, but shall believe that these things which he saith shall come to pass; he shall have whatsoever he saith. Therefore I say unto you, what things soever ye desire, when ye pray believe that ye receive them, and ye shall have them." The key here is verse 22. (HAVE FAITH IN GOD). More precisely put your trust, your faith fully in what God's word says knowing that it is true and God's word does not change. If you can do that then you will move in faith knowing that God cannot and will not fail. If you lack faith of yourself and in yourself that is fine. Put your faith in God and His Word where it belongs and doubt not.

As we conclude our short chapter on faith turn to Romans 5:1-2. "Therefore being justified by faith, we have peace with God through our Lord Jesus Christ: By whom also we have access by faith into His Grace wherein we stand and rejoice in hope of the glory of God." If your intention is truly to Abide in the Vine you cannot enter into that abiding relation without faith nor will you receive justification or experience His grace upon your life. We can never live or move or have our being in Christ Jesus unless we live and walk by faith.

Chapter VI
"The Living Word!"

Our understanding of the written word of God and our relationship and depth of understanding of the Living Word are possibly the most vital elements of our abiding relationship with the Lord, Himself. Unlike a footrace, a motocross or a border-crossing race in white water on a river-board the race we find ourselves in here in this life is one we must win because there is not another race tomorrow.

The word race appears four times in the written word. The first is in Psalm 19:5 and it is the Hebrew word [orach] which means a well trodden road or familiar path. The second is the Hebrew word [merowts] which appears in Ecclesiastes 9:11 and means literally a run or trial of speed. The third word is in I Corinthians 9:24 and is the Greek word [stadion] from which we derive the word stadium which is a fixed distance such as a set race course. And the last is found in the book of Hebrews chapter 12 and verse 1 and is the Greek word [agon] which is a contest filled with anxiety, conflict and contention involving effort or fight. And agon is derived from the root word [ago] which means to lead, to bring forth or to carry.

Bear with me for a minute as we diverge slightly but we will come back shortly to these scriptures and see the importance of each as we travel the river of life at face level. I want to begin by looking at the Gospel of Luke the 24th chapter and verses 44-48, "And He said unto them, These are the words which I spake unto you while I was yet with you, that all things must be fulfilled, which were written in the law of Moses and in the prophets, and in the psalms, concerning Me. Then opened He their understanding, that they might understand the scriptures.

And said unto them, Thus it is written, and thus it behoved Christ to suffer, and to rise from the dead the third day: And that repentance and remission of sins should be preached in His name among all nations, beginning at Jerusalem. And ye are witnesses of these things." Now hold the thought that Jesus was here referring to certain scriptures which spoke of His suffering, death and resurrection and the proclaiming of God's truth so that men and women everywhere might come to repentance and receive salvation and eternal life. Now look at John 1:1-9. "In the beginning was the Word and the Word was with God and the Word was God. The same was in the beginning with God. All things were made by Him and without Him was not anything made that was made. In Him was life and the life was the light of men. And the light shineth in darkness and the darkness comprehended it not. There was a man sent from God whose name was John. The same came for a witness, to bear witness of the Light, that all men through Him might believe. He was not that Light but was sent to bear witness of that light. That was the true Light, which lighteth every man that cometh into the world."

Now you may have read that portion of scripture a hundred times and not thought too much about it, and you might have just brushed over it this time, but we must not take this scripture lightly, but instead see it through God's eyes for what it is really saying to us. Jesus is the Living Word. And as such He changes not. He always has been and He will always be. Every word written in the Bible speaks of Christ in some way or it speaks of our relationship to Him. It speaks of His Godliness, our ungodliness, His Holiness, our unholiness. He said when speaking to Moses from the burning bush, "Tell them I AM hath sent you." And to the Pharisees He said, "Before Abraham was I AM." He also said, "I am the way,the truth, the life, the same, the door, the Good Shepherd, I come to give you life and that more abundantly. And we could go on and on and on. We need to realize that when we read the Word of God we are actually reading God. It is not a comic book or fairy tail or a story about some character who lived and died. You are actually reading the life of God. Jesus is the living all encompassing Word!

If people were to read you what would the words of your life and reality say?

John said the following in relationship to the written word regarding Christ. John 20:30-31. "And many other signs truly did Jesus in the presence of His disciples which are not written in this book: But these are written, that ye might believe that Jesus is the Christ, the Son of God; and that believing ye might have life through His name." and John 21:25, "And there are also many other things which Jesus did, the which if they should be written every one, I suppose that even the world itself could not contain the books that should be written. Amen"

Can any mortal comprehend all God has done and the depth of His love for His creation? I think not. It is beyond us to know and understand the magnitude of His greatness but the Living Word spoke through the written word as the Holy Spirit moved upon man to write down what we have, to draw us to an abiding relationship with our Creator, and our Creator came to bring us an understanding of the greatness of His love and to give us a glimpse of His Holiness and the depth of our depravity that we would recognize our need of salvation.

I was recently talking with a former teacher of mine now in her 90s who spoke of a time in her life when she didn't think she needed to be saved. She hadn't committed murder or adultery or fornicated or stolen but when God revealed Himself to her she said she realized her sin was in her failure to follow God fully. And how true that is of all mankind. Now I'm not going to get off on a teaching of the Ten Commandments here for there have been many excellent books written on that topic. I just want to say God's Word, the Living Word says there are none righteous no not one.

OK, now that you all think I forgot about the race and those four scriptures, let's go back and see what this race we find ourselves in is all about and discover how we can draw closer to Christ in the abiding relationship He wants with each of us, "for all things were made by Him and for Him and without Him was not anything made that was made." If you think for a moment that the things which concern you are not important to the Lord then you have not even begun the journey with Him in the river of life and have a long way to go to enter into the abiding relationship He wants with you.

Let's look at the 19th psalm and as we do, and from here on, look at the entire word as it reveals Christ and our need of Him. Psalm 19 reads, "The heavens declare the glory of God and the firmament sheweth His handywork. Day unto day uttereth speech and night unto night sheweth knowledge. There is no speech nor language where their voice is not heard. Their line is gone out through all the earth, and their words to the end of the world. In them hath He set a tabernacle for the sun. Which is as a bridegroom coming out of his chamber; and rejoiceth as a strong man to run a race. His going forth is from the end of the heaven, and his circuit unto the ends of it: and there is nothing hid from the heat thereof. The law of the Lord is perfect, converting the soul; the testimony of the Lord is sure making wise the simple. The statutes of the Lord are right rejoicing the heart: the commandment of the Lord is pure, enlightening the eyes. The fear of the Lord is clean, enduring for ever: the judgements of the Lord are true and righteous altogether. More to be desired are they than Gold, yea, than much fine gold: sweeter also than honey and the honeycomb. Moreover by them is thy servant warned: and in keeping of them there is great reward.

Who can understand his errors? cleanse thou me from secret faults. Keep back thy servant also from presumptuous sins; let them not have dominion over me: then shall I be upright, and I shall be innocent from the great transgression. Let the words of my mouth, and the meditation of my heart, be acceptable in Thy sight, O Lord, my strength, and my redeemer."

Some day if the Lord allows I want to write a book on the 19th psalm. It is so full and rich in the truth of God's word and its effect upon us. Each verse is a chapter in itself. If the saying is true that a picture is worth a thousand words, then these few words of imagery describing God's works and words have painted a magnificent picture or might I say a glorious portrait of our Lord.

Within this short psalm His greatness is shown, His creation revealed, His righteousness held high and the effect of His word upon His creation boldly proclaimed. He has traveled that road from one end to the other and Knows it well. If we allow Christ to be our guide, in the race we are in, we shall not stumble. As we keep our eyes on Him and abide in Him we shall gain strength, for this race through life, from the Bridegroom, the Strong Man, who has run the race before, Whose going forth is from eternity to eternity. The race we are in has been well traveled by God. We are not alone.

Now let's look at Ecclesiastes 9:10-11. "Whatsoever thy hand findeth to do, do it with thy might; for there is no work, nor device, nor knowledge nor wisdom, in the grave, whither thou goest. I returned, and saw under the sun, that the race is not to the swift, nor the battle to the strong, neither yet bread to the wise, nor yet riches to men of understanding, nor yet favor to men of skill: but time and chance happeneth to them all."

Remember, the word for race, in verse eleven, means; - a run or a trial of speed. But the race is not to the swift according to verse 11 so how do we run the race? We run it with diligence, commitment, faithfulness, zeal and hard work. So we are running a well traveled road which we commit to do with all our heart, soul, mind and strength.

Look with me now at I Corinthians 9:24-27. The word for race in verse 24 is the Greek word 'stadion' which means a fixed distance or set course. The course we are running is set by God and is straight and narrow but it also has obstacles. "Know ye not that they which run in a race run all, but one receiveth the prize. So run, that ye may obtain. And every man that striveth for the mastery is temperate in all things. Now they do it to obtain a corruptible crown but we an incorruptible. I therefore so run, not as uncertainly; so fight I not as one that beateth the air: But I keep under my body, and bring it into subjection: lest that by any means, when I have preached to others, I myself should be a castaway."

Like any race course there is a beginning point and an ending point. We begin that race the moment we accept God's free gift of salvation and we end it when we are received up into glory. If, as you run a race you are constantly looking at those around you instead of being focused on the course ahead you will never win a race and you will be likely to trip over obstacles and not even finish the race. In the same way, as we enter the race in the river of life, if we take our eyes off of our guiding Light, Jesus Christ, we will find ourselves stumbling over the obstacles that come our way and fail to finish! When we train in the natural we must put aside those things that would hinder us and bring our body into obedience. In the race of life it is important that our spirits are in control not the flesh. Paul knew the importance of running that race in the Spirit for he strove to obtain an incorruptible crown. Without a close relationship in the 'Word of God' with 'The

Word', Jesus Christ, we cannot complete that race. We cannot enter in without Him.

Now our last scripture in regards to the race we are in is Hebrews 12:1-4, "Wherefore seeing we also are compassed about with so great a cloud of witnesses, let us lay aside every weight and the sin which doeth so easily beset us and let us run with patience the race that is set before us. Looking unto Jesus the author and finisher of our faith who for the joy that was set before Him endured the cross despising the shame, and is set down at the right hand of the throne of God. For consider Him that endured such contradiction of sinners against Himself, lest ye be wearied and faint in your minds. Ye have not yet resisted unto blood striving against sin."

If you recall, the word for race here is 'agon' which is a contest involving anxiety, conflict, and contention requiring effort and fight on our part in order to win. So here we are in this race in the river of life faced with tribulation and we are to run it with patience, [tribulation worketh patience], and lay aside all hinderances and sin. Notice it says we are to put aside, or away, the sin which easily besets, [causes us to fail]. We can't do that without setting our eyes on Jesus Christ who is the author and finisher of our faith. The wages of sin is death. We have not resisted sin unto blood but He endured the cross for us. If you try to run the race alone, the end result is death, but if you run it while abiding with Christ the debt has been paid and the end is eternal life.

Just what is this race and how do we compete in it? It is well traveled and our Lord has traveled it from beginning to end. He knows and understands every obstacle that you or I will face. It is a trial of speed and we are only given so much time on this earth and only God knows how much time we will have, and yet we are not to hurry through it but instead be diligent and faithful to do all as unto the Lord, as we compete and endure this race. The race is also a set course, straight and narrow, designed by God, to be run in the Spirit for the crown that awaits us is incorruptible and finally this race is filled with obstacles, conflict, anxiety and contention. It isn't an easy road. We are in a battle, a fight to the finish and we cannot finish the race without setting our eyes upon our guide who has run the race before having been victorious over death and hell and removed those things from our path, only as we accept the free gift of eternal life and abide in Him and thereby turn from sin and finish strong the race we are in. So now that we understand the race we are in let's look a little closer at our Lord and learn to understand Him as the "Living Word".

Return with me to John ! and let's see if we can't begin to develop an abiding relationship with a deeper understanding of the Living Word. John 1:1 reads, "In the beginning was the Word. And the Word was with God and the Word was God." As we learn of the Word we must always remember that Jesus Christ is the Living Word. In the beginning was Jesus! "And the Word was with God." [Jesus was with God.] "And the Word was God." [Jesus was and is God]! Now look at Genesis 1:1. "In the beginning God created the heaven and the earth." It says, "In the beginning God." Before the start of time God was and is. Jesus was and is God and has existed eternally forever. Part two says God created the heaven and the earth. [The Word which is and was God and was and is Jesus Christ created the heaven and the earth]. Now look at Genesis 1:2-3. And the earth was without form and void and darkness was upon the face of the deep. And the Spirit of God moved upon the face of the waters. And God said Let there be light and there was light." In the beginning of time when God created, the earth was empty and darkness was over the face of the waters. But God Said, 'The Word' said, Let there be light. Jesus is the Word and Jesus is God and the Word Spoke and light came forth and dispelled darkness. Now let's go back to John and read John 1:2-4. "The same was in the beginning with God. All things were made by Him, and without Him was not anything made that was made. In Him was life and the life was the light of men."

Now don't any of you reading this misquote me and think that I am making a case for the doctrine of Jesus Only for I firmly believe and teach the validity of the Trinity, [Father, Son and Holy Spirit]. But here we are dealing with the Living Word and I want us to understand His importance and our need to intimately know and understand all He is and did and does! Keeping that in mind, let's proceed. The Word was with and was and is God. Jesus, the Word [Himself] by means of the Holy Spirit,[God's Spirit], [the Spirit of Christ], moved upon the face of the waters creating all that the Word spoke. And when it says in the Word or within Christ was life and that life was the light of men, it is saying that apart from Christ there is no life nor is there light to dispel darkness. The life within the Word, within God, within Christ is the light of man. So when the Word spoke in the beginning, God the Word, Christ, fully entered into His Creation and the darkness that was in the world can never overcome, can never control nor eliminate the light for it is God's life in His Creation. Verse 5 of John 1 reads, " And the light shineth in darkness and the darkness comprehended it not." Now if we return to Genesis 1 and continue to read the creation story we see the total involvement of the Light within creation and that along every step of the way we hear God, the Word saying of the creation, it is good. In verse 27 of Genesis 1 we read, "So God created man in His own image, in the image of God created He him: male and female created He them." In verse 26 God, the Word, said, "Let us make man in Our image after Our likeness. So in these two verses we see the oneness of God and the plurality of the Trinity of God the Father, the Son or Word and God the Holy Spirit. Then in chapter two of Genesis we see the actual creation process God went through to create man and *verse 7 reads, "And the Lord God formed man of the dust of the ground and breathed into his nostrils the breath of life and man became a living soul." Remember that verse four of John 1 said that within the Word, within God, within Christ was life and that life was the light of man. When God breathed the breath of life into man God was imparting His very life into man and that life came to enlighten man. When man sinned darkness didn't overcome the light, it simply blinded man to the truth of the light which was the life of God. When the Son of God, the Word of God, was born into His creation, lived among His creation and shined as the light of His creation, most of His creation rejected the Creator choosing to remain in darkness. That darkness tried to put out the light, to extinguish it, to kill it, to nail THE LIGHT to a cross but the Word had already said, 'If I be lifted up I will draw all men unto Me and on the third day that light shined forth brighter than ever. Verses 9-13 of John 1 say the following speaking of the Word, The Living Word Jesus Christ, "That was the true Light which lighteth every man that cometh into the world. He was in the world and the world was made by Him and the world knew Him not. He came unto His own , and His Own received Him not. But as many as received Him to them gave He power to become the sons of God, even to them that believe on His name. Which were born, not of blood, nor of the will of the flesh, nor of the will of man, but of God."*

Now because those who have received the life of Christ the Word, have received His light, we are told in Matthew 5:14-16, "Ye are the light of the world. A city that is set on an hill cannot be hid. Neither do men light a candle and put it under a bushel, but on a candlestick; and it giveth light unto all that are in the house. Let your light shine before men, that they may see your good works and glorify your Father which is in heaven." Through your acceptance and ongoing relationship with the Living Word, the life and light of Christ is meant to shine unto all the world and dispel the darkness within the hearts of mankind.

When God through the Living Word spoke to Moses from the burning bush and told him who He was, He said [I AM] revealing His character showing that He is all in all. Jesus said before Abraham was [I AM]. The Great I AM is the Way, the Truth, the Life, the Light, the Door, the source of all that is good, the Awesome God, the Creator, the Saviour, Redeemer, Healer and we could go on and on and on and never completely cover all that is included in the great I AM.

But even though we can't completely cover all that the Living Word encompasses I do want to look at a number of scriptures more so let's turn to II Timothy 3:16-17. "All scripture is given by inspiration of God and is profitable for doctrine, for reproof, for correction, for instruction in righteousness: That the man of God may be throughly furnished unto all good works."

Now let's not forget the Living Word is God and as such will always express something of His person or relationship with His creation, His Holiness or our lack of it or His purpose for 'His Creation'. Here in II Timothy we are made to understand that every word [every scripture] recorded in the book [the Bible] is a direct revelation from God as the Holy Spirit moved upon men to write it down in the same way that when God [The Word] spoke in creation the Spirit moved upon the face of the waters and all was created. All is recorded for our benefit that we might learn from it the wonderful things of God and turn from error of our ways unto righteousness, doing so, we should become perfect and complete in all we should do.

Matthew 5:17-19 reads this way, "Think not that I am come to destroy the law or the prophets. I am not come to destroy but to fulfill. For verily I say unto you. Till heaven and earth pass one jot or one tittle shall in no wise pass from the law till all be fulfilled. Whosoever therefore shall break one of these least commandments, and shall teach men so shall be called the least in the kingdom of heaven, but whosoever shall teach them, the same shall be called great in the kingdom of heaven."

Let's break this down. If Jesus,[The Word] had come to do away with the law or the prophets, [the written word or the spoken word], He would be destroying the very essence of His Person and thereby be a house divided. Instead He came to be the fulfillment of His word or in actuality fulfilling the very purpose he had set for His coming as a man. The very next thing the Living Word spoke of the word was that until heaven and earth should pass away not one point of punctuation would cease to exist from the law, [the written word], until all of the recorded or written word is fulfilled. In other words nothing written of or in the Word will ever change. God [The Word] is the same yesterday, today and forever. God [The Living Word] changes not. Therefore if we break any of the teachings of the word and teach others that any part of the revealing of [The Word] is irrelevant we shall be called the least in the Kingdom because we shall be denying some of the purpose and character of the [Living Word]. But on the other hand if we are doers of 'The Word' living and being and walking in the word, thereby growing in the very nature of God and shall teach others to live of the same we shall be called the greatest in the Kingdom. This is what it truly means to abide in the Vine, [The Lord, The Word] and allow, the Word's words to abide in you! The deeper our understanding, the greater becomes our walk and the more we become, as His disciples like the Master. In other words there is true evidence of our being disciples of the "WORD".

II Corinthians 3:5-8 tells us, "Not that we are sufficient of ourselves to think any thing as of ourselves but our sufficiency is of God: Who also hath made us able ministers of the new testament; not of the letter, but of the Spirit; for the letter killeth, but the Spirit giveth life. But if the ministration of death written and engraven of stones was glorious, so that the children of Israel could not steadfastly behold the face of Moses for the glory of his countenance, which glory was done away: How shall not the ministration of the Spirit be rather glorious?"

You and I apart from a true abiding, intimate relationship with Jesus Christ are insufficient within ourselves so that we are incapable of accomplishing anything of value for God. It is only through Him and our becoming one with Him that we are capable of becoming effective ministers of the things of God. He it is who has made us able ministers of the new testament, established in His shed blood, not of the letter [the written unbending law] but of the Spirit [the essence or purpose of the "LIVING WORD" given by the Holy Spirit of God] for the written unbending law brings death but the essence or purpose behind the letter given by the Holy Spirit revealing the Living Word gives life!

Remember this, that even the Law written in stone [the Ten Commandments written by the hand of God and given to Moses] was glorious. It was such in that it showed man"s inability to be holy enough to live up to the Holiness of God and the necessity of a saviour. At the same time because of Moses' intimacy with God, God's glory was seen for a time upon his face but that glory was but a glimpse of the glory that was to come for the reflected glory would be done away with even as Moses himself would die but the glory that comes through the filling of the Spirit of the Living God who leads us into all truth as He reveals the Living Word is truly glorious for the glory of God is seen in and through our lives as we daily become more like Him.

Psalm 19:7 reads, "The law of the Lord is perfect converting the soul: the testimony of the Lord is sure, making wise the simple." Everything that is written is perfect, complete, mature and whole and it is through our understanding and agreement with that, that the soul is converted from death to life, brought out of darkness and filled with the light of the Lord. All that the Lord spoke is fixed permanently and changes not bringing wisdom to all who would hear and receive.

In the 119th psalm there are a number of verses I wish to look at. They are as follows. Psalm119:89-91, 105, 114 and 116. "For ever, O Lord, Thy Word is settled in Heaven. Thy faithfulness is unto all generations; Thou hast established the earth; and it abideth. They continue this day according to Thine ordinances; for all are Thy servants ....Thy Word is a lamp unto my feet and a light unto my path ....Thou art my hiding place and my shield: I hope in Thy Word .... Uphold me according unto Thy Word that I may live: and let me not be ashamed of my hope."

Please, I cannot emphasize enough that the Word is with God and the Word is God. It is not just someone's ideas about God. The Word is forever established, permanently dwelling in heaven. All that the Word has revealed of God and all that the Word has created is a permanent abiding part of God and His creation. His faithfulness is forever, His creation is His servant and every aspect and every portion of that creation is subject to the ordinances God has established to govern His creation by 'The Word'.

When God says through the scripture that His Word is a lamp unto our feet and a light unto our path He is not simply speaking of His recorded word but more precisely The Living Word, for the Living Word [Jesus Christ] is the light that enlightens all mankind who will openly receive Him. God is my shield, my protector, my hiding place and He will preserve me from all trouble. It is in His Word that I place my hope. There is nothing of God [The Word] that will ever change; and I can fully trust in Him; in the Word. If my hope is in Him I am certain that The Word will truly uphold me as long as i am living in and abiding in 'The Word'!

Deuteronomy 8:3 reads, "And He humbled thee and suffered thee to hunger and fed thee with manna, which thou knewest not neither did thy fathers know; that He might make thee know that man doth not live by bread only but by every word that proceedeth out of the mouth of the Lord doth man live."

We are told that physical nourishment is only a small part of life for life consists of the physical, the soul and the spiritual life and the purpose of life is revealed through all the Living Word spoke to create and reveal Himself and His purposes for His creation. Later Jesus [The Word] says that He was the true Manna which fed them in the wilderness, He was the Water and much more. A true abiding relationship can only come by The Word totally abiding within the individual seeking to abide in Christ.

In John 14:21,23-24 we read, "He that hath My commandments and keepeth them, he it is that loveth Me; and he that loveth Me shall be loved of My Father and I will love him, and will manifest Myself to him .... If a man love Me, he will keep My words, and My Father will love him and We will come unto him and make our abode with him. He that loveth Me not keepeth not My sayings: and the Word which ye hear is not mine; but the Father's which sent Me."

It is not simply enough to receive the commandments; teachings, words of, the Lord. We must live of them; they must abide within us. It is through this that we show our love to Him. It is in this we are loved of the Father and the Son makes Himself known to us. It is in and through the keeping of the words of [The Word] that the Father and the

Son make their home within our earthen vessels. If we fail to keep the words or sayings of the Son we show our lack of love for the Son who is the revealed fullness of the Godhead through the Word of the Father. Jesus is here expressing both His oneness with the Father and His submission unto the Father.

In John 15:9-10 we read, "As the Father hath loved Me so have I loved you; continue ye in My love. If ye keep My commandments, ye shall abide in My love; even as I have kept My Father's commandments and abide in His love." At this point the 'Living Word' proclaims the eternal love of God: Who is Love; for His Son, and the Son's love for His creation. At the same time He is encouraging you and I to continue in His love. This can only occur through our keeping the Son's or [The Word's] commandments in the same way the Son kept and fulfilled the Father's commandments. It was through that obedience that He abided in the love of the Father and it is in our obedience to [The Word] that we abide in His love!

In the epistle of James 1:23-25 this is written, "For if any be a hearer of the Word, and not a doer, he is like unto a man beholding his natural face in a glass; For he beholdeth himself, and goeth his way, and straightway forgetteth what manner of man he was. But whoso looketh into the perfect law of liberty, and continueth therein, he being not a forgetful hearer, but a doer of the work, this man shall be blessed in his deed."

Please, I beg of you remember The Word is God. If we hear God and don't live according to His set purposes for us as His children we foolishly go our own way missing the blessings He intends us to have, but if we hear [The Word] and live of [The Word] we shall be blessed in all we do.

II Timothy 2:15 says, "Study to shew thyself approved unto God, a workman that needeth not to be ashamed, rightly dividing the Word of truth." God,The Word, says that we are to study [The Word] learn of God Himself that we will never need to be ashamed because of mishandling or misapplying God's teachings. We will always rightly divide [apply and teach] the Word of Truth. Jesus is the Word and He is the Truth. In order for this to happen we must walk in truth, abide in Him and His word always abide in us. I have known a number of people who have memorized a great deal of scripture and were able to quote large portions verbatim but who lacked understanding of the truth because they had never developed an abiding relationship with [The Word] That abiding relationship is ever so important.

Isaiah 55:10-11 reads, "For as the rain cometh down, and the snow from heaven, and returneth not thither, but watereth the earth, and maketh it bring forth and bud, that it may give seed to the sower and bread to the eater: So shall My word be that goeth forth out of My mouth: it shall not return unto Me void, but shall accomplish that which I please, and it shall prosper in the thing whereto I sent it."

As it is in the natural establishing of all the Word created bringing the ongoing physical results God intended that His creation would be provided for through the fulfillment of that which was created by The Word; so will the Spiritual results be as the word goes forth spoken by whomsoever [The Word chooses to use and the use of the word spoken by God through man will not return to [The Word] empty but it will prosper [have the intended effect for which it was sent forth].

Ephesians 6:14-17 reads, "Stand therefore, having your loins girt about with truth, and having on the breastplate of righteousness, and your feet shod with the preparation of the gospel of peace; above all, taking the shield of faith, wherewith ye shall be able to quench all the fiery darts of the wicked. And take the helmet of salvation and the sword of the Spirit which is the Word of God."

Since our next chapter is on the equipping I am not going to break this down here except to say [The Word] tells us that our offensive weapon, which is sharper than any two edged sword, the Sword of the Spirit, is the Word of God. Remember the misuse of the written word [The Law] can and will bring death while the correct use of the Sword of the Spirit will bring life. I cannot emphasize enough the importance of [The Word] abiding within.

As we conclude this chapter look at Hebrews 4:12. "For the word of God is quick and powerful, and sharper than any two edged sword, piercing even to the dividing asunder of soul and spirit, and the joints and marrow and is a discerner of the thought and intents of the heart. [The Word] Jesus Christ knows you inside and out and is capable of doing what ever is needed to make us into His image. ABIDING IN THE VINE REQUIRES INTIMATELY KNOWING [THE WORD]!

Chapter VII
"Fully Equipped"

One of the most important things in running white water, whether raft, kayak or river-board is proper equipment. My sons are sticklers for this and for all involved being properly trained. Without being fully equipped and properly trained in the use of protective gear your life would be in grave jeopardy from multiple dangers that come against you as you attempt to maneuver around and over and through obstacles as you travel the physical white water at face level.

It is even more dangerous, and you are in greater jeopardy of harm, in the spiritual race living at face level in the river of life, if you are not fully equipped and trained in the use of your equipment. We have touched on much of our equipping in the first six chapters. By now we should understand that we cannot live at face level in the river of life alone. We must have a deep abiding relationship with the Lord. Neither can we run the race from the shore. We must enter into the water and become fully immersed in all that entails.

There are times in this life when we feel that we are alone in the race as we battle to make it through the many rapids we face. Be assured that once you begin that race with Christ you have never been and never will be alone. He has promised that He will never leave you nor forsake you. And since [The Word] is forever settled in heaven and God is not a man that He should lie and He is the same yesterday, today and forever, you are never alone. How difficult it is sometimes even when you know He is right there to function in faith and understand He cares. Even His first disciples, who lived and walked with Him and knew His physical presence, often failed to understand His concern for them and His protection. Look at Mark 4:35-41. "And the same day, when the even was come, He saith unto them. Let us pass over unto the other side. And when they had sent away the multitude, they took Him even as He was in the ship. And there were also with Him other little ships. And there arose a great storm of wind, and the water beat into the ship so that it was now full. And He was in the hinder part of the ship asleep on a pillow; and they awake Him, and say unto Him, Master, carest Thou not that we parish? And He arose, and rebuked the wind, and said unto the sea,"Peace" be still. And the wind ceased, and there was great calm. And He said unto them, Why are ye so fearful? how is it that ye have no faith? And they feared exceedingly, and said one to another. What manner of man is this, that even the wind and the sea obey Him?"

Have you ever known that God was with you in your time of need but felt He was asleep? And then when you saw Him work in the situation you failed to understand? My dear friends, our Lord, who never sleeps and never forsakes us would say unto us, "Why are you so fearful? how is it that you have no faith?" Then there are those times when you can't see Him or sense His presence at all. It is much like learning to run rapids on a river-board and your instructor has disappeared into a rapid ahead of you and you feel totally alone and surrounded by danger. Are you able to make it through? Have you learned your lessons? Are you properly equipped to face the challenge? Look at John 6:15-21. "When Jesus therefore perceived that they would come and take Him by force, to make Him a King, He departed again into a mountain Himself alone. And when even was now come, His disciples went down unto the sea, and entered into a ship, and went over the sea toward Capernaum. And it was now dark, and Jesus was not come to them. And the sea arose by reason of a great wind that blew. So when they had rowed about five and twenty or thirty furlongs, they see

Jesus walking on the sea, and drawing nigh unto the ship and they were afraid. But He said unto them, It is I, be not afraid. Then they willingly received Him into the ship and immediately the ship was at the land whither they went." Now Mark in his gospel adds some additional details in Mark 6:47-48, And when even was come, the ship was in the midst of the sea, and He alone on the land. And He saw them toiling in rowing for the wind was contrary unto them and about the forth watch of the night He cometh unto them, walking upon the sea and would have passed by them." And Matthew also adds even greater detail in Matthew 14:28-33. "And Peter answered Him and said, Lord, If it be Thou, bid me come unto Thee on the water. And He said come. And when Peter was come down out of the ship, he walked on the water, to go to Jesus. But when he saw the wind boisterous, he was afraid; and beginning to sink, he cried saying, Lord, save me. And immediately Jesus stretched forth His hand, and caught him, and said unto him, O thou of little faith wherefore didst thou doubt? And when they were come into the ship, the wind ceased. Then they that were in the ship came and worshipped Him saying, Of a truth Thou art the Son of God."

We need to notice here that the disciples were physically apart from Jesus when they found themselves struggling against the elements which could destroy them, but notice also that Jesus saw their struggle and went unto them to be there if they should only ask. Notice also that He would have passed by totally in control of the situation but not removing the struggle from them but waiting for them to act in faith. Having before seen the power and authority of God which He had given unto them they still didn't understand the relationship between the physical and the spiritual. When Peter got a glimpse of the spiritual authority of Jesus, he , functioning in the Spirit, began to walk on water but upon seeing the physical danger quickly lost sight of the true and living God and the equipping he had in his relationship with Christ, and he began to sink. It was only after Jesus reached out to Peter and caught him and said, O thou of little faith wherefore didst thou doubt? that they were again able to focus upon the solution to the danger they faced. And only when Christ was again in the ship with them did the wind cease and they worshipped Him for who He was.

Tell me why we are so quick to be fearful and doubt and feel all alone when we can't see God and then in total despair cry out for help. And when He delivers us we worship Him but soon forget again. Is it the fact that we have yet to understand the equipping God has provided and the victory already won? Is it that we have yet to understand the authority we have in our relationship in the Lord? Could it be we don't yet understand the full purpose and operation of the equipment we are given to do battle against all obstacles we face in our race in the river of life at face level? What ever the reasons, we will fail often until we reach the point of perfection through our ongoing commitment to the abiding life in Jesus Christ, that we become like Him. The purpose of every challenge we face is to make us more like Him and to increase our faith to make us productive for the Kingdom of God.

Now I know many of you are asking yourselves, why did I use the scriptures I just used when we had discussed them in chapter V on faith? My answer is this. You should have been able to glean one thing from those scriptures on faith in chapter V and my hope is that you were able to gain something else from them here as an introduction to being fully equipped. And if that is true then our repetition has value. So now let's look at how God equips us to do battle in the river of life we travel.

First of all He has given us certain gifts which are only useful if used and not placed upon a shelf somewhere as a trophy to be looked back at and recalled only at certain times. Romans 2:1-8 says, "I beseech you therefore brethren, by the mercies of God, that ye present your bodies a living sacrifice, holy' acceptable unto God, which is your reasonable service. And be not conformed to the world but be ye transformed by the renewing of your mind. That ye may prove what is that good and acceptable, and perfect will of God. For I say, through the grace given unto me, to every man that is among you, not to think of himself more highly that he ought to think, but to think soberly, according as God hath dealt to every man the measure of faith. For as we have many members in one body, and all members have not the same office; So we being many, are one body in Christ, and every one members one of another. Having then gifts differing according to the grace that is given to us, whether prophecy, let us prophesy according to the proportion of faith; Or ministry, let us wait on our ministering; or he that teacheth, on teaching; or he that exhorteth, on exhortation: he that giveth, let him do it with simplicity; he that ruleth, with diligence; he that sheweth mercy, with cheerfulness."

Before God supplies us with gifts to help us navigate the course set before us it is important that we present our bodies fully unto Him and separate ourselves from the ways of the world. It is only in doing that, that we can prove what is that good and acceptable and perfect will of God. And just what is the will of God for us? First of all it is that we be saved and filled with His Spirit and totally separated from the things of the world. If we try to navigate the river of life and enter those waters while hanging on to all the baggage of the old life that baggage will weigh us down and pull us under keeping us from living at face level. So the old ways have to go in order to be replaced by the new.

Now when it comes to the gifts God gives each of us, some are the same but some are distinct in that we all have slightly different things we will face and slightly different purposes within the body but we are all in the same race. For instance, what God has given you can help me in areas where I lack and I might be gifted where you lack but all are necessary in helping others enter in and complete the race. No man is an island unto himself. We all need one another in the body of Christ. On the other hand as we travel through this life there will be many times you will find yourself alone and it is important that you understand all the Spiritual gifts God has provided and the Spiritual equipping He has fitted you with and know when and how to use them.

Keep this in mind as we look closely at three portions of scripture: I Corinthians 12:7-11; Ephesians 4:7-11 and Ephesians 6:10-18. I Corinthians 12:7-11 says, "But the manifestation of the Spirit is given to every man to profit withal. For to one is given by the Spirit the word of wisdom: to another the word of knowledge by the same Spirit; To another faith by the same Spirit; to another the gifts of healing by the same Spirit: To another the working of miracles; to another prophecy; to another discerning of spirits; to another divers kinds of tongues: But all these worketh that one and the selfsame Spirit, dividing to every man severally as He will."

Please take note that the individual gifts make up the total manifestation of the gifts of the Spirit and are given unto man to profit with all, [that is all of the gifts]. God never intended that each individual would be limited to the use of only one or two gifts. When it says that He, [The Holy Spirit],gives one gift to one and another gift to another it does not mean that those gifts are passed out and if the one receiving the gift is not present when that gift is needed to operate that faith wont operate or healing or miracles, etc. How ridiculous would that be. That would greatly limit the power of God. Verse 11 tells us that all the gifts belong to the Holy Spirit and work through the Holy Spirit as He distributes or works each gift through a man or woman of His choosing when the manifestation of a particular gift is needed. We are to be available to be used in all the gifts and we are told in 13:31 to covet or desire the best gifts. These gifts are given and meant for us to be effective in the service and furthering of the Kingdom.

Then in Ephesians 4:7-11 we are told, "But unto every one of us is given grace according to the measure of the gift of Christ. Wherefore He saith, when He ascended up on high, He led captivity captive, and gave gifts unto men. (Now that He ascended, what is it but that He also descended first into the lower parts of the earth? He that descended is the same also that ascended up far above all heavens, that He might fill all things.) And He gave some, apostles, and some prophets; and some evangelists, and some, pastors and teachers;" Now Ephesians 4:12-16 gives the purpose for which these gifts are given. "For the perfecting of the saints, for the work of the ministry, for the edifying of the body of Christ till we all come in the unity of the Faith, and the knowledge of the Son of God, unto a perfect man, unto the measure of the stature of the fulness of Christ: That we henceforth be no more children tossed to and fro, and carried about with every wind of doctrine by the slight of men, and cunning craftiness, whereby they lie in wait to deceive; But speaking the truth in love, may grow up into Him in all things which is the Head, even Christ: From Whom the whole body fitly joined together and compacted by that which every joint supplieth, according to the effectual working in the measure of every part, making increase of the body unto the edifying of itself in love."

The leadership gifts of the church are given to the church to build the church; win the lost, reach the world for Christ, and bring the Saints to maturity through the preaching and teaching of the word so that the Saints of God can do the work of the ministry so that the entire body of Christ will be edified. And that through edification the body of Christ will be unified in faith and unified in the knowledge of the Son of God so that each and every child of God will become full and mature in the stature and fulness of Christ: Apostles, Prophets, Evangelists, Pastors and Teachers are given to the body to provide leadership, encouragement, direction, learning and equipping so that all would no longer be tossed to and fro, and carried about with every wind of doctrine or change that comes along and the lies and deception that are there to destroy in much the same way that rapids in a river may appear harmless but be very deceptive and unless you fully understand the function of the rapids you face they can cause great harm. God has provided leadership to teach the truth and protect you from harm so that you grow up understanding and speaking the truth in love so that the whole body of Christ is effective in every way and is furnished and edified in love.

We need to understand that we are not simply in a race but that we are actually in a battle and that the enemy is determined to keep us from finishing that race and he will attack us from all directions with whatever he can throw at us and with all the force and furry he can generate. Since we are in a life and death battle as we travel through this life, God has not left us vulnerable, but has provided us with the proper equipment to do battle and reach victoriously the end of the race.

Ephesians 6:10-18 covers our battle and military issue, "Finally, my brethren, be strong in the Lord, and in the power of His might. Put on the whole armour of God, that ye may be able to stand against the wiles of the devil. For we wrestle not against flesh and blood, but against powers, against the rulers of the darkness of this world, against spiritual wickedness in high places. Wherefore take unto you the whole armour of God, that ye may be able to withstand in the evil day, and having done all, to stand. Stand therefore, having your loins girt about with truth, and having on the breastplate of righteousness. And your feet shod with the preparation of the gospel of peace;

above all, taking the shield of faith wherewith ye shall be able to quench all the fiery darts of the wicked. And take the helmet of salvation and the sword of the Spirit, which is the Word of God: Praying always with all prayer and supplication in the Spirit, and watching thereunto with all perseverance and supplication for all saints;"

First we are told to be strong in the Lord and in the power of His might. We are not simply admonished to be strong, for our strength is no match for our enemy, but we are told to be strong in our Lord's strength and power. We need to always be aware that it is in Him that we live and move and have our being and also that apart from Him we can do nothing, but through Christ you can do all things. Second we are told to put on His armour. God's armour is especially designed for the battle we face on a daily basis. Our battle isn't against flesh and blood. If it were our equipment would be quite different. Sometimes we feel the battle is against flesh and blood but the force behind those battles is the spiritual realm of darkness at work in the world in which we live. This is the fight for life we are in and this is why we must take the whole armour of God. It is not enough to only take part of the armour or only what you think you will need or are comfortable with. In order to stand in the day when evil comes upon you, you must have taken, learned how to use and confidently applied to your life all God has provided and become battle ready. Apart from that when the battle rages you will fall and become a casualty of war. We must vigorously come against our enemy facing him head on at face level not simply holding our ground but as we do battle taking over. Our enemy knows our vulnerability and if we try to fight him in our own strength he will quickly strike any and all weaknesses. Since our Lord created us He knows how to cover and protect every aspect of our lives. We are to stand upon the rock, Christ Jesus. Then He tells us to have our loins girt about with His truth. In the natural your loins are an extremely vulnerable and weak area of the battle in which a single well placed blow can bring great pain, harm or death. In the spiritual battle it is a target that can give in to much temptation. In the spiritual battle in which we find ourselves the enemy launches multiple attacks in three areas. They are; the lust of the flesh, the lust of the eyes, and the pride of life. Your loins encompass the procreative aspect of your being and much of the sexual avenue of temptation. We are admonished to girt our loins with God's Truth. As we put on Christ we put on truth. He is truth and as we are faithful to apply the truth of God's word we will not give in to those things which would make us susceptible to sexual sin. We are also told to have on the breastplate of righteousness. The Breast is what we consider the center of the will and emotions of man for it is out of the heart that the mouth speaks and it is from the heart of man that wickedness or evil devises are planned. It is vital that the seat of our will and emotions which can easily be turned to unrighteousness be clothed with His righteous. Notice that it is His Breastplate of righteousness not our own for our righteousness is as filthy rags so we exchange our righteousness for His righteousness. It is interesting that in a battle our feet are shod with the gospel or 'good news' of peace. The victory has already been won. It is just that our enemy doesn't know it. Everywhere we go and in the heat of battle we walk in the peace of God shod with the Good News that no mater what, that peace is ours. In order to stop every fiery dart that comes against us and stop the enemies darts and render them useless we are given the shield of faith. God's word says we are victorious, we are free, we are saved, He is our protector, He is our shield. My faith might lack but His does not. He has provided the shield of faith. Next we are to take the helmet of salvation. Our thought life is protected through salvation. We are not to be doubtful or fearful but bravely wear the helmet as we do battle. As we do so we need understand that we are protected from the the thoughts that come and the attacks the enemy launches against our mind. Next we are to take the Sword of the Spirit which is the Word of God. No attack can overcome the word. Jesus is the Word . The Word became flesh and dwelt among us and He it is Who fights for us and finally we are told to pray with all prayer and supplication with perseverance for all Saints, praying in the Spirit. So as we put on Christ and pray in the Spirit we complete our being fully equipped for the Spirit knows what to pray for and how to pray when we don't and the entire Godhead who has already won the battle fights for us. You lack nothing!

Chapter VIII
"No Turning Back"

There are many who begin the race and are desirous of being victorious and finishing the race but for one reason or another they never finish the race. They leave the race and turn aside to other things. They may start out fast with their eyes intently focused on the Lord and the prize but soon tire of the journey and long for the old ways. we need to remember that the race is not to the swift or the battle to the strong but it is to the committed that obtains the victors crown. If you turn back and walk away God says you are not worthy of the call. It is unfortunate that many are called but few chosen. Actually the call is to all who will hear and heed and the chosen is determined by those who choose to faithfully follow. The thought that some are chosen and others are set apart for destruction would make God an unfair and unjust God, for all are created in His likeness and He would not want any to perish. The fact that there are those who seem to be predestined for destruction is simply the fact that God knows ahead of time who will follow and accept the free gift and who will reject and go the way of the world. So how do we know who is a true believer and who is not? When God sent Moses to lead His people out of Egypt into the promise land they all saw the mighty hand of God in power and judgement upon Pharaoh and all Egypt and there were a great many of the Egyptians who seeing the hand of God and the miracles who left Egypt with the Children of Israel but when things got tough they began to long for the leeks and garlic of Egypt as did many of the Hebrews, and all were stirred up to murmur against Moses and the God they saw in power but didn't know. It quickly became apparent that they were a long way from knowing and understanding the God of Abraham and abiding and trusting in Him. There were multitudes that came out of Egypt and a great number because of unbelief perished in the wilderness over the forty years of seeing God's provision, power, healing and deliverance and hearing His word. Today the church needs to heed a warning and lesson from the wilderness wanderings that just because you walk in the presence of the righteous and say all the right things and see God move doesn't mean that you are growing and abiding in Christ.

Let's look at some scripture verses in Exodus and see if we might be subject to some of the same. Exodus 14:10-12 says, "And when Pharaoh drew nigh, the children of Israel lifted up their eyes, and behold, the Egyptians marched after them; and they were sore afraid, and the children of Israel cried out unto the Lord. And they said unto Moses, Because there were no graves in Egypt, hast thou taken us away to die in the wilderness? wherefore hast thou dealt thus with us, to carry us forth out of Egypt? Is not this the word that we did tell thee in Egypt, saying, Let us alone, that we may serve the Egyptians? For it had been better for us to serve the Egyptians, than that we should die in the wilderness."

The minute they saw danger they wanted out and started complaining. If you have entered into white water and suddenly decide it was better in the calm water you can gripe but you will find it more dangerous to try to swim out of the rapid than to follow your teacher or guide through it. Had they tried to turn back to Egypt, at the point where they were , Pharaoh would have had no mercy upon them, and as they followed God through the Red Sea it wasn't just 'smooth sailing', it was on Dry Land. When they reached the other side of the Red Sea unharmed and saw the armies of Pharaoh drowned in the Red Sea they rejoiced in the deliverance and worshipped and praised the Living God. But it was only a matter of days and they again began to murmur and complain and looked back to

Egypt. Why is it that Satan has been able to deceive man into thinking that a full belly with persecution is better that the presence of God with victory? Look at Exodus 16:1-4. "And they took their journey from Elim and all the congregation of the children of Israel came unto the wilderness of Sin, which is between Elim and Sinai on the fifteenth day of the second month after they departed out of the land of Egypt. And the whole congregation of the children of Israel murmured against Moses and Aaron in the wilderness. And the children of Israel said unto them, would to God we had died by the hand of the Lord in the land of Egypt, when we sat by the flesh pots and when we did eat bread to the full: for ye have brought us forth into this wilderness to kill the whole assembly with hunger. Then said the Lord unto Moses, Behold, I will rain bread from heaven for you, and the people shall go out and gather a certain rate every day that I may prove them whether they will walk in My law, or no."

It is a strange thing that they cried unto God in Egypt when the heavy hand of the Egyptians were upon them and God heard their cry and sent Moses to be their deliverer. And now all they remember is having full bellies and forget the heavy burdens and scourgings and wish to return. In the same way many people begin in the race in the river of life enjoying the blessings and presence of God and the minute they face any problem or lack of provision they want to return to their old ways forgetting what they have been redeemed from. No matter how great the miracles of God or the abundance of His blessings man is prone to forget and Satan will quickly remind us of what we thought was good in the old sinful life and blind our eyes to the truth.

So it was there that God provided the manna from heaven and fed them to the full and provided manna for them for forty years in the wilderness. As soon as they began to journey out of the wilderness of Sin grumbling began again. Look at Exodus 17:1-3. "And all the congregation of the children of Israel journeyed from the wilderness of Sin, after their journeys, according to the commandment of the Lord, and pitched in Rephidim and there was no water for the people to drink. Wherefore the people did chide with Moses, and said, Give us water that we may drink. And Moses said unto them, Why chide ye with me? Wherefore do ye tempt the Lord? And the people thirsted there for water; and the people murmured against Moses and said, Wherefore is this that thou hast brought us up out of Egypt to kill us and our children and our cattle with thirst." And again God speaks to Moses and provides for their thirst.

Oh how quickly the people who saw God's blessings daily, when they couldn't see God or the servant of God, turned to creating their own devices and making their own gods. It is still the same today as it was then. In Exodus 32:1, we read, "And when the people saw that Moses delayed to come down out of the mount the people gathered themselves together unto Aaron, and said unto him. Up make us gods which shall go before us for as for this Moses, the man that brought us up out of the land of Egypt, we wot not what is become of him."

With people today when it seems like God isn't there or they don't get an immediate answer people grow tired of waiting or serving God who doesn't fit their plans and want to make God into their image or after their design instead of the other way around.

In II Timothy 2:3-4 we are told in Paul's admonition to Timothy, which holds true for us today, the following, "Thou therefore endure hardness, as a good soldier of Jesus Christ. No man that warreth entangleth himself with the affairs of this life; that he may please him who hath chosen him to be a soldier." Whether we face problems or setbacks or hardships or can't see God or hear Him we don't desert our post or choose another leader. Our command doesn't change and until we receive new orders from the Lord we stay our course.

In Matthew chapter 13 Jesus told the parable of the Sower and later explained its' meaning to the disciples. Look at Matthew 13:18-23. "Hear ye the parable of the sower. When any one heareth the word of the kingdom, and understandeth it not, then cometh the wicked one and catcheth away that which was sown in his heart. This is he which received seed by the wayside. But he that received the seed into stoney places, the same is he that heareth the word and anon with joy receiveth it: Yet hath he not root in himself, but dureth for a while: for when tribulation or persecution ariseth because of the word, by and by he is offended. He also that received seed among the thorns is he that heareth the word; and the care of this world and the deceitfulness of riches, choke the word, and he becometh unfruitful. But he that receiveth seed into the good ground is he that heareth the word, and understandeth it; which also beareth fruit, and bringeth forth some an hundredfold, some sixty some thirty." Has the fallow ground of your heart been broken up? And have you turned from the things of the world? If this world still has a hold on you, you will be unfruitful and if your heart is not pliable you will not be able to endure hardships or persecution and if you are still standing looking in you will never understand the word. In all three cases it isn't that hard to turn back. Little disappointments can cause small grumblings which become large rumblings, which cause you to leave the race course.

In Matthew 24:4-13 we are told that many will fall away and even betray one another before the return of Christ. How many will leave the race before the end? Look at verses 4-13. "And Jesus answered and said unto them, take heed that no man deceive you. For many shall come in my name saying I am Christ; and shall deceive many. And ye shall hear of wars and rumours of wars; see that ye are not troubled for all those things must come to pass, but the end is not yet. For nation shall rise against nation, and kingdom against kingdom; and there shall be famines and pestilences and earthquakes, in divers places. All these are the beginning of sorrows. Then shall they deliver you up to be hated of all nations for my name's sake. And then shall many be offended and shall betray one another, and hate one another. And many false prophets shall rise and shall deceive many. And because iniquity shall abound the love of many shall wax cold. But he that shall endure unto the end the same shall be saved." As I was writing this chapter I was made aware of the 8.9 quake and the tsunami in Japan that has just claimed thousands of lives. It is so important that we turn not back but endure unto the end. Christ's return could be any day now or before I finish this book or if you are reading it before you finish. Before I could return to writing this, war had broken out in Libya and we, [the United States, Canada, UK and France] were bombing Libya for their attack on Israel. It could very well be that this book never gets finished, but remember the verses we just read said that these are but the beginnings of sorrows for the end is not yet.

Now stay with me as we go to II Timothy 3:1-5. "This know also, that in the last days perilous times shall come for men shall be lovers of their own selves, covetous, boasters, proud, blasphemers, disobedient to parents, unthankful, unholy. Without natural affection, trucebreakers, false accusers, incontinent, fierce, despisers of those that are good, traitors, heady, high minded; lovers of pleasure more than than lovers of God: Having a form of godliness, but denying the power thereof: from such turn away." I don't know when I have ever seen this on a world wide scale in the history of man after the flood in which God destroyed the earth and only saved eight souls; at the level I see it today. If there are those of you who are greater historians out there than I and wish to correct me on that, feel free.

Now look at II Timothy 4:1-5, and read Paul's charge to Timothy. "I charge thee therefore before God, and the Lord Jesus Christ, who shall judge the quick and the dead at His appearing and His Kingdom; Preach the word; be instant in season, out of season: reprove, rebuke, exhort with all longsuffering and doctrine. For the time will come when they will not endure sound doctrine; but after their own lusts shall they heap to themselves teachers having itching ears; and they shall turn away their ears from the truth and shall be turned unto fables. But watch thou in all things, endure afflictions, do the work of an evangelist, make full proof of thy ministry." False doctrines and teaching are rampant and any attempt at correcting those errors is met with great resistance. Have we entered the time when the teaching of the truth of the Gospel of Jesus Christ will find it almost impossible to reach the lost? Is it the time when many will fall away? Are we seeing the time when many would make their own gods instead of receive the true God? Will many leave the race they were so zealous to complete because those around them will not follow the true directions so they will say, "Why keep going I've done enough". Don't give up and don't look back. Only those who endure to the end can win the race.

But what if you do fail? What if the rapids get too strong and you head to shore and look for calmer water? Is it possible to fail and be restored and again enter the race? Or is the race over? Can you stumble and fall and pick yourself up and start all over again? WELL, BE ENCOURAGED. Proverbs 24:16 says, "For a just man falleth seven times and riseth up again: but the wicked shall fall into mischief." If you began the race with Jesus Christ, He will do all in His power to see that you finish it. Nothing and no one else can take you out of the race. Only you can remove yourself from the running and He is not about to let that take place. John Mark who went with Paul and Barnabas to minister, at a certain point turned back. Look at Acts 13:13. "Now when Paul and his company loosed from Pamphylia: and John departing from them returned to Jerusalem." Paul was very unhappy with Mark's leaving and on a later journey when Barnabas wanted to take him with them again Paul was not of a mind to do so and Paul and Barnabas parted ways but did John mark actually re-enter the race and make it to the end. Was he restored and able to endure all he would face? In Paul's second letter to Timothy we get a glimpse of Mark's restoration. Read II Timothy 4:9-11. Do thy diligence to come shortly unto me: For Demas hath forsaken, having loved this present world, and is departed unto Thessalonica; Crescens to Galatia, Titus unto Dalmatia. Only Luke is with me. Take Mark and bring him with thee; for he is profitable to me for the ministry." Paul was locked in a Roman prison expecting shortly to face death and this scripture would indicate that not only did Mark return to the race but that he was in the race for the prize of the high calling in Christ and that He had become a fruitful , productive minister of the gospel and it was Paul's desire to have him with Him and continue to grow in the things of the Lord. Yes it is possible to return to the race and finish as a faithful productive abiding disciple of Jesus Christ, but much time is lost, much production is lost and many blessings you would have received fall by the wayside. But know this even though there are things that are lost that can be restored there are other things that will never be restored and grieving the Holy Spirit who lives within you,[Whose temple you are}, weakens the communion you are meant to have with Him and the abiding relationship you have worked so hard to obtain by abiding in the Vine and having the Word of God abiding in you.

I John 1:5-10 reads, "This then is the message which we have heard of Him, and declare unto you, that God is light, and in Him is no darkness at all. If we say that we have fellowship with Him, and walk in darkness, we lie and do not the truth: But if we walk in the light, as He is in the light, we have fellowship one with another, and the blood of

Jesus Christ His Son cleanseth us from all sin. If we say that we have no sin, we deceive ourselves, and the truth is not in us. If we confess our sins. He is faithful and just to forgive us our sins, and to cleanse us from all unrighteousness. If we say that we have not sinned, we make Him a liar, and His Word is not in us."

No man is without sin. God says we have all sinned and come short of His glory, but He also says we are being changed from glory to glory into His image. He never gives up on making us into His image but it requires that we walk in the light and remain in the race. If we find ourselves swept aside into sin and having turned from the race course, we need to confess of our sins and receive His forgiveness and get back in the race. I John 2:1-6 says, "My little children, these things write I unto you, that you sin not. And if any man sin, we have an advocate with the Father, Jesus Christ the righteous; And He is the propitiation for our sins: and not for ours only, but also for the sins of the whole world. And hereby we do know that we know Him, if we keep His commandments. He that saith I know Him, and keepeth not His commandments, is a liar, and the truth is not in him. But whoso keepeth His word, in him verily is the love of God perfected: hereby know we that we are in Him. He that saith he abideth in Him ought himself also so to walk, even as He walked." It is God's intention that we never fail or fall and that we always abide and that we walk as He walked and that we are always fruitful. If you have failed then get up and repent and get back in the race. You are not the first to fail nor the first to find forgiveness. He will continue to change you from glory to glory into His image and the love of God will be perfected in you as you abide in Him.

Another guarantee that we can be restored is the fact that we have a High Priest who is always making intercession for us! Look at Hebrews 7:25. "Wherefore He is able to save them to the uttermost that come unto God by Him, seeing He ever liveth to make intercession for them." and Hebrews 13:5 reads,"Let your conversation be without covetousness; and be content with such things as ye have : for He hath said, I will never leave thee nor forsake thee." And Romans 8:35-39 says, "Who shall separate us from the love of Christ? shall tribulation, or distress or persecution or famine, or nakedness, or peril or sword? As it is written, For thy sake we are killed all the day long; we are accounted as sheep for the slaughter. Nay, in all these things we are more than conquerors through Him that loved us. For I am persuaded, that neither death, nor life, nor angels, nor principalities, nor things present, nor things to come, nor height, nor depth, nor any other creature, shall be able to separate us from the love of God, which is in Christ Jesus our Lord." On Christ's behalf He never leaves us and always watches over us. Only we can turn our backs upon Him but to do so is almost impossible for once you have come to Jesus and been filled with the Holy Spirit and sealed unto the day of redemption no man can in his heart turn and deny all that the Lord has done and truly believe that the things the Lord has done in and through your life by the working of the Holy Spirit were of the devil. We are given a warning in Hebrews 6:4-6 and Hebrews 10:26-29 and also know that God will allow many to perish,[Romans 9:21-23] but Hebrews 6:9 and II timothy 2:19-21 show the near impossibility of total loss of salvation once you have received.

Look at each of these with me if you would. Hebrews 6:4-6 reads, "For it is impossible for those who were once enlightened, and have tasted of the heavenly gift, and were made partakers of the Holy Ghost, and have tasted the good word of God, and powers of the world to come. If they shall fall away, to renew them again unto repentance, seeing they crucify to themselves the Son of God afresh and put Him to an open shame." Now this is speaking of those who have moved in the miraculous power of God and have not just fallen into sin where there is forgiveness, but who have totally rejected Christ and literally blasphemed the Holy Spirit which is the only thing that is unforgivable. Hebrews 10:26-29 says, "For if we sin willfully after that we have received the knowledge of the truth, there remaineth no more sacrifice for sins, But a certain fearful looking for of judgement and fiery indignation, which shall devour the adversaries. He that despised Moses law died without mercy under two or three witnesses; Of how much sorer punishment suppose ye, shall he be thought worthy, who hath trodden under foot the Son of God, and hath counted the blood of the covenant, wherewith He was sanctified an unholy thing, and hath done despite unto the Spirit of grace?" If this were speaking of one sin then I John would be meaningless as well as every scripture on repentance and forgiveness. What it is speaking of is a willful continuance of sin and rejection of the truth and refusal to repent and be forgiven. Romans 9:21-23 reads, "Hath not the potter power over the clay, of the same lump to make one vessel unto honour, and another unto dishonour? What if God, willing to shew His wrath, and to make His power known endured with much longsuffering the vessels of wrath fitted to destruction: And that He might make known the riches of His glory on the vessels of mercy, which He had afore prepared unto glory." **Now on the outset of that portion of scripture it looks like some are destined for hell and others destined for heaven from the beginning but that is not the case.** *God would not have any to perish but He knows who will accept the free gift and who will reject but being a vessel of honor or dishonor is the choice of the vessel. Notice the scripture is not speaking of separate lumps of clay but the same lump that the potter makes into a vessel for honor or a vessel of dishonor. The making process requires the yielding on the part of the vessel. We as vessels either yield to the master's hand or we resist the molding of our lives by the hand of the Lord. II Timothy 2:19-21 says, "Nevertheless the foundation of God standeth sure, having this seal. The Lord knoweth them* *that are His. And , let every one that nameth the name of Christ depart from iniquity. But in a great house there are not only vessels of gold and of silver, but also of wood and of earth and some to honour and some to dishonour. If a man therefore purge himself from these, he shall be a vessel unto honour, sanctified, and meet for the master's use, and prepared unto every good work." And Hebrews 6:9 says, speaking of falling away, "But, behold, we are persuaded better things of you, and things that accompany salvation, though we thus speak." Paul cries out the warning of turning our backs upon the Lord and crucifying Him afresh but also points out that those in Christ are sealed and we need to turn from sin and walk in the Spirit. Can you get back in the race and finish strong? Yes - Do it!*

Chapter IX
"Facing Your Fears"

One of the most difficult things about finishing the race whether it is getting back in the race after failure or simply continuing through a rough and difficult section of a race course, in the natural, or facing difficult times in your life, is facing your fears and overcoming. Now there is one fear that is good and that is the honest fear of the Lord for that brings wisdom, knowledge and understanding in the things of God. But there are many fears that weaken and destroy you and keep you from completing the course set before you and finishing the race victorious and in joy. There are a great many fears that come upon us as we live in this world and press toward the mark of the high calling in Christ Jesus! If you have ever failed there is fear of not being accepted back and fear of rejection, also fear of failing again. Even if you have never failed there is always fear of rejection, acceptance and failure that can plague any and all. Then there are fears of sickness, disease, and failing health or fear of death, fear of man, fear of tests, fear of heights, fear of the dark, fear of water, fear of animals, fear of being alone and many other fears that can strike you in one way or another. Fears are abundant and take on many forms. We could go on and make a list so long that it would never end. But if I did that I would only give you another fear; the fear of a never ending list and we would never get to the point of the chapter of facing your fears and "I"M AFRAID I WOULD LOSE MOST OF YOU AS READERS". So what does God say about fears and how we are to face them and overcome them?

I could take all the fear nots that appear in the Bible and simply say don't fear anything but just telling someone don't, doesn't always get you through dangerous rapids or over massive boulders. When dangers, real or imagined cause you to fear they can paralyze you to the point where you can't see or hear anything else. God's people in the Bible were faced with many fears; some real, some imagined. How they faced those fears determined how they either overcame them or gave into them and it didn't matter how great or victorious they had been in life. Elijah, one of God's greatest prophets, whom God took home to glory, bypassing death and leaving earth on a fiery chariot; after great victory over the prophets of Baal on Mt. Carmel ran from the wicked Queen Jezebel feeling all alone and helpless, fearing for his life. When God finally appeared to him, He informed him that he wasn't alone, that the Lord had 7,000 who had not bowed a knee to Baal and again gave him work to do.

Was Elijah's fear real? God had protected him, fed him and mightily used him during 3 1/2 years when it didn't rain and had given him power to slay 400 false prophets, call fire down from heaven, out run King Ahab's chariot and many other mighty miracles; but in a moment of weakness he forgot who it was that was his shield and buckler, his high tower and who it was who was in control of his life. So if Elijah could give in to fear is it strange that Satan has been able to cause so many hearts to fail because of fear?

But then we see Elijah's predecessor, Elisha with a double portion of the Anointing of the Holy Spirit that was upon Elijah doing twice as many recorded miracles as Elijah and never succumbing to fear or depression. But then Elisha's servant, seeing things in the natural gave in to fear until Elisha prayed that God would open his eyes to see in the Spirit. Take a look at II Kings 6:15-23. "And when the servant of the man of God was risen early, and gone forth, behold, an host compassed the city both with horses and chariots. And his servant said unto him. Alas, my master! how shall we do? And he answered, Fear not: for they that be with us are more than they that be with them. And

Elisha prayed, and said, Lord, I pray Thee, open his eyes, that he may see. And the Lord opened the eyes of the young man; and he saw; and, behold, the mountain was full of horses and chariots of fire round about Elisha. And when they came down to him, Elisha prayed unto the Lord, and said, smite this people, I pray thee, with blindness. And He smote them with blindness according to the word of Elisha. And Elisha said unto them. This is not the way, neither is this the city; follow me and I will bring you to the man whom ye seek. But he led them to Samaria. And it came to pass, when they were come into Samaria, that Elisha said, Lord open the eyes of these men, that they may see. And the Lord opened their eyes, and they saw; and behold, they were in the midst of Samaria. And the king of Israel said unto Elisha, when he saw them, My father shall I smite them? shall I smite them? And he answered, Thou shalt not smite them: wouldest thou smite those whom thou hast taken captive with thy sword and with thy bow? Set bread and water before them, that they may eat and drink, and go to their master. So the bands of Syria came no more into the land of Israel." The servant of Elisha, when his eyes were opened, was able to overcome his fear because he saw through the eyes of God and was able to see the numbers of God's army, but Elisha had an ongoing intimate abiding relationship with the Lord that allowed him to overcome all fear knowing that the Lord was always with him.

Now these fears may be extreme cases in comparison to the fears that most face but let's look at other fears found in the word and as we do we will discover that they are very much like we face on a daily basis.

In Isaiah 21:4 we read, "My heart panted, fearfulness affrighted me, the night of my pleasure hath he turned into fear unto me." Isaiah portrays here the intensity of fear of the future if Babylon should fall. Even though Israel was subservient to Babylon they feared a worse more ruthless nation could rule over them. Have you ever faced sudden fear when hearing about war in some place and had your heart beat out of your chest. This type of fear causes many to succumb to heart attacks.

In Mark 5:33 we see a completely different kind of fear. Look with me at that scripture. "But the woman fearing and trembling, knowing what was done in her came and fell down before Him, and told Him all the truth." Now this woman who had an issue of blood for twelve years had had faith to believe if she but touched Jesus clothes she would be healed, but when she was and Jesus said who touched me she feared she had done something wrong and that she shouldn't have done what see did and was now in trouble. Fear of having done wrong and fear of disapproval is a very common and real fear but in this case her actions were not wrong and the Lord praised her for her faith and spoke peace unto her.

The next two scriptures we are going to look at are actually fear of the unknown. Anything we don't understand or can't explain we have a tendency to fear. This can be anything, from our first day in school, moving to a new area, meeting new people, our first date, driving a car or flying or going into space, or as with Jesus followers being confronted by angels or having Jesus appear unto you. In Matthew 28:1-8 we read, "In the end of the Sabbath , as it began to dawn toward the first day of the week, came Mary Magdalene and the other Mary to see the sepulchre. And behold, there was a great earthquake: for the angel of the Lord descended from heaven, and came and rolled back the stone from the door and sat upon it. His countenance was like lightning, and his raiment white as snow; And for fear of him the keepers did shake and become as dead men. And the angel answered and said unto the women, Fear not ye, for I know that ye seek Jesus which was crucified. He is not here, for He is risen, as He said. Come see the place where the Lord lay. And go quickly, *and tell His disciples that He is risen from the dead: and behold, He goeth before you into Galilee, there shall ye see Him: lo I have told you. And they departed quickly from the sepulchre with fear and great joy and did run to bring His disciples word." And we read Matthew 14:26 these words. "And when the disciples saw Him walking upon the sea they were troubled, saying, It is a spirit; and they cried out for fear."*

Now in the case of those guarding the tomb they had every reason to fear and the angel didn't dispel their fears, but he did dispel the women's fears even though they still left fearing the unknown but obeying and when met by Jesus their fears were gone. The same thing held true for Jesus walking on water. Thinking He was a ghost they were afraid and only when they knew it was Jesus did their fear cease but not totally for when Peter, who stepped out on the water in faith, looked around and saw the waves, he began to sink and began to fear and cry out for help. Fear will never fully cease until we understand what it means to be one with the Lord and fully abide in the Vine.

Another common fear of mankind is the fear of man. It begins even in a little baby. A strange look from a stranger will cause a baby to cry. The bully in school can drive fear into the heart of a boy or girl so that they don't want to go to school. Then there is the fear of a boss or co-worker, fear of stockers and gangs and fear of waring nations. Look at the following scriptures which are just a few commands to not fear man. Proverbs 29:25, "the fear of man bringeth a snare: but whoso putteth his trust in the Lord shall be safe." Psalm 56 reads, "Be merciful unto me, O God: for man would swallow me up; he fighting daily oppresseth me. Mine enemies would daily swallow me up: for they be many that fight against me, O Thou Most High. What time I am afraid, I will trust in thee. In God I will praise His word, in God I have put my trust; I will not fear what flesh can do unto me. Every day they wrest my words; All their thoughts are against me for evil. They gather themselves together, they hide themselves, they mark my steps, when they wait for my soul. Shall they escape by iniquity? in Thine anger cast down the people, O God. Thou tellest my wanderings: Put Thou my tears into Thy bottle: are they not in Thy book? When I cry unto Thee, then shall mine enemies turn back: this I know; for God is for me. In God will I praise His Word: in the Lord will I praise His Word. In God have I put my trust: I will not be afraid what man can do unto me. Thy vows are upon me, O God; I will render praise unto Thee. For Thou hast delivered my soul from death: wilt not Thou deliver my feet from falling. That I may walk before God in the light of the living?" And Psalm 118:6. "The Lord is on my side; I will not fear: what can man do unto me?" and finally we turn to Luke 12:4-7. "And I say unto you my friends, Be not afraid of them that kill the body, and after that have no more that they can do. But I will forewarn you whom ye shall fear: fear Him, which after He hath killed hath power to cast into hell; yea I say unto you, Fear Him. Are not five sparrows sold for two farthings, and not one of them is forgotten before God? But even the very hairs of your head are numbered. Fear not therefore: ye are of more value than many sparrows."

The psalmist understood that fear is a snare. It binds you and holds you captive. Even though we are not specifically told I believe that this psalm was written by David and he knew what it was like to be hated, stocked, lied about, pursued and have attempts made upon his life but he was not going to give in to fear. He also knew that by putting his trust in God there was safety and mercy and that the Lord bottled up his tears and always heard his cry and did battle for him. Then Jesus told us in Luke, don't fear man who can only kill the body, fear God who after death can cast into hell. And in verse seven of chapter twelve he tells us that we are important to the Lord so fear not.

Let's stay in chapter 12 of Luke and look at a few more fear nots. Luke 12:22-23 and 28-32 read this way, "And He said unto His disciples, Therefore I say unto you, take no thought for your life, what ye shall eat; neither for the body what ye shall put on. The life is more that meat and the body more than raiment. ....And seek not ye what ye shall eat or what ye shall drink, neither be ye of doubtful mind. For all these things do the nations of the world seek after and your Father knoweth that ye have need of these things. But rather seek ye the kingdom of God: and all these things shall be added unto you. Fear not, little flock: for it is your Father's good pleasure to give you the Kingdom."

Here Jesus, who in verse seven told us not to fear man because we are of value, now tells us not to fear or be concerned about our needs for he knows our needs and instead we are to move from the natural to the spiritual and realize that the answer to all our fears come through our spiritual inheritance of the kingdom of God and it is that, that we should seek after. As we press into the kingdom, which if you are in Christ, you have been translated into and press toward the mark of the high calling of God in Christ Jesus and abiding relationship in the Vine and the Word which is Jesus Christ, all fear will leave you for it is God's desire to give you the kingdom of God and everything that entails.

Another major fear that keeps many from going through the race in the river of life in an attitude of faith, trust and peace of heart is the fear of death; whether it is fear of dying young or simply fear of death itself and pain and suffering or what awaits them. Let's look at the following scriptures which deal with this issue. Proverbs 10:27 reads, "The fear of the Lord prolongeth days: but the years of the wicked shall be shortened." and Proverbs 14:26-27 says, "In the fear of the Lord is strong confidence and His *children shall have a place of refuge. The fear of the Lord is a fountain of Life, to depart from the snares of death." Proverbs 19:23 reads, "The fear of the Lord tendeth to life: and he that hath it shall abide satisfied; he shall not be visited with evil." and Psalm 23:4 says, "Yea, though I walk through the valley of the shadow of death, I will fear no evil: for Thou art with me; Thy rod and Thy staff they comfort me." And Hebrews 2:14-15 reads, "Forasmuch then as the children are partakers of flesh and blood, He also Himself likewise took part of the same; that through death He might destroy him that had the power of death, that is, the devil; and deliver them that through fear of death were all their lifetime subject to bondage."*

All the scriptures we just looked at make it very clear that the fear of death and the snares that draw you into death can be avoided or overcome by the fear of the Lord. The fear of the Lord brings a confidence that causes you to overcome the fear of death and prolongs your days. Even if you are walking in the very shadow of death you need not fear evil because the Lord is with you and as you trust in Him, He will bring comfort. And if and when you should die remember He says, "Precious in the sight of the Lord is the death of His saints." Psalm 116:15. And if you have a fear of dying young remember you have an added promise in Ephesians 6:1-3. "Children, obey your parents in the Lord: for this is right. Honour thy father and mother, which is the first commandment with promise; That it may be well with thee, and thou mayest live long on the earth." Also look at one more scripture on conquering or overcoming the fear of death. In Exodus 14:11-14 it reads thus. "And they said unto Moses, Because there were no graves in Egypt, hast thou taken us away to die in the wilderness? wherefore hast thou dealt thus with us, to carry us forth out of Egypt? Is not this the word that we did tell thee in Egypt saying, Let us alone, that we may serve the Egyptians? For it had been better for us to serve the Egyptians, than that we should die in the wilderness. And Moses said unto the people, fear ye not, stand still, and see the salvation of the Lord which He will shew you to day: for the Egyptians who you have seen to day, ye shall see them again no more for ever. The Lord shall fight for you, and ye shall hold your peace." Why is it that people are so given over to fear that they can't understand God's deliverance and have no understanding of what salvation really provides and what it means to abide in Christ and rest in His Love. Instead, when faced with fears of death they can't see what they have been delivered out of and want to go back into bondage. Fear is bondage. God says don't fear, stand still and see God's salvation. Hold your peace, He is fighting for you. In other words, Shut up and watch God work. [My rendition.] He is on the throne and in control simply recognize the fact and trust in Him to fight for you. If your fear of death, danger, sickness and disease is so strong that you are unable to stand still and trust, you will end up double minded and turn from God, and if you do all you fear will come upon you for your fears of man and natural occurrences are greater than your fear of God. Look at Deuteronomy 28:58-66 and then Proverbs 1:23-30. " If thou wilt not observe to do all the words of this law that are written in this book, that thou mayest fear this glorious and fearful name, THE LORD THY GOD: Then the Lord will make thy plagues wonderful and the plagues of thy seed even great plagues and of long continuance. Moreover He will bring upon thee all the diseases of Egypt, which thou wast afraid of: and they shall cleave unto thee and every sickness, and every plague which is not written in the book of this law, them will the Lord bring upon thee until thou be destroyed. And ye shall be left few in number where as ye were as the stars of heaven for multitude, because thou wouldest not obey the voice of the Lord thy God. And it shall come to pass, that as the Lord rejoiced over you to do you good, and to multiply you: so the Lord will rejoice over you to destroy you, and to bring you to naught: and ye shall be plucked from off the land whither thou goest to possess it. And the Lord shall scatter thee among all people, from the one end of the earth even unto the other: and there thou shalt serve other gods, which neither thou nor thy fathers have known even wood and stone. And among these nations shalt thou find no ease neither shalt the sole of thy foot have rest; But the Lord shall give thee there a trembling heart an failing of eyes and sorrow of mind. And thy life shall hang in doubt before thee, and thou shalt fear day and night and shalt have none assurance of thy life." And look at Proverbs 1:23-30. "Turn you at my reproof: behold I will pour out My Spirit unto you. I will make known My Words unto you, Because I have called, and ye refused, I have stretched out My hand and no man regarded; But ye have set at naught all My counsel and would none of My reproof: I also will laugh at your calamity; I will mock when your fear cometh; When your fear cometh as a whirlwind when distress and anguish cometh upon you. Then shall they call upon me, but I will not answer; they shall seek Me early, but they shall not find me. For that they hated knowledge and did not choose the fear of the Lord: They would none of My counsel. They despised all my reproof." The Lord has provided a way of overcoming and being victorious when fears come but if man does not take the way provided and learn to fear God, destruction will come like a whirlwind; calamity will fall upon you, your hearts shall fail you and your minds be troubled and disease shall cleave unto you until you are destroyed in death. But this is not what the Lord desires for us. He has provided salvation for us and poured out His Spirit unto us and given us His word. He simply asks that we would fear Him and learn of His ways and trust fully in Him. As we do, fear will leave.

Other fears that plagued the people of God and the New Testament believers and you and I today, as we are living in this world traveling in the river of life, and involved in the race set before us, are as follows: Financial, fear of falling, fear of destruction, fear of the dark and night, lack of sleep, sudden fear or panic attacks, fear of wicked men, fear of the end of the world, fear of heart failure, climate change, earthquakes, tornados, hurricanes, tidal waves, tsunamis, fear of standing for Christ and witnessing because of others: Fear of reprisal for standing for the truth and what is right and fear of perishing. But God gives answers to overcome all these fears and any other you might have. Lets look at some more scriptures and then add the rest of His fear not answers and reasons for overcoming our fears.

To start with look at Proverbs 3:13-26. "Happy is the man that findeth wisdom. and the man that geteth understanding. For the merchandise of it is better that the merchandise of silver, and the gain thereof of fine gold. She is more precious than rubies: and all the things thou canst desire are not to be compared unto her. Length of days is in her right Hand and in her left hand riches and honour. Her ways are ways of pleasantness and all her paths are peace. She is a tree of life to them that lay hold upon her. The Lord by wisdom hath founded the earth, by understanding hath He established the heavens. By His knowledge the depths are broken up, and the clouds drop down the dew. My son, let not them depart from thine eyes: keep sound wisdom and discretion. So shall they be life unto thy soul and grace to thy neck. Then shalt thou walk in thy way safely, and thy foot shall not stumble. When thou liest down, thou shalt not be afraid: yea, thou shalt lie down, and thy sleep shall be sweet. Be not afraid of sudden fear, neither of the desolation of the wicked when it cometh. For the Lord shall be thy confidence and shall keep thy foot from being taken."

As you draw into the abiding relationship with the Lord and His word, you will gain through the knowledge of His word and your intimacy with Him, the understanding that you need not fear anything. He will keep you from harm. You will have long life and abundance of blessings and honor bestowed upon you. Fear robs you of all God has for you.

It is the thief that comes to steal, kill, and destroy and fear is one of his strongest weapons against God's children but Jesus Christ came to bring life more abundantly. As you grow in the word of God, which is your 'true food', your eyes will be opened to all of His promises and He will truly become your confidence. You can have sweet sleep, for "He giveth His beloved sleep", and not fear. Even in the middle of attacks upon you by the wicked you shall know peace. "My peace I leave with you", said Jesus, and panic attacks shall not come upon you, "For perfect love casts out fear". Your intimacy with Christ assures you, as the Spirit of God dwells within and you walk in the Spirit and live by the faith of the Son of God who gave Himself for you, that you shall always have that perfect love within, for nothing can separate you from the love of God which is in Christ Jesus our Lord.

Now turn to Luke 21:25-28. "And there shall be signs in the sun and in the moon, and in the stars; and upon the earth distress of nations with perplexity: the sea and the waves roaring; Men's hearts failing them for fear, and for looking after those things which are coming on the earth for the powers of Heaven shall be shaken and then shall they see the Son of man coming in a cloud with power and great glory. And when these things begin to come to pass then look up and lift up your heads; for your redemption draweth nigh."

Devastating 'natural' disasters have greatly increased and hurricanes and tidal waves and tsunamis have taken many lives. The seas are indeed roaring and nations are indeed perplexed not knowing how to cope with all that is happening and with more and more films being made of the end of the world men's hearts are indeed failing them for fear. These things have begun but fear not it's time to look up and lift your heads high for your redemption draweth nigh and the King of Glory, our Saviour and Lord, Jesus Christ shall soon appear and every eye shall behold

Him and every knee shall bow and every tongue shall confess that Jesus Christ is Lord.

I want us to look at these next three scriptures together for they can rob us of great blessings meant to be ours, and can keep us from being fruitful as we continue racing in the river of life. The three scriptures I want to look at are John 19:38-40, II Timothy 1:6-10 and John 20:19. John 19:38-40 reads, "And after this Joseph of Arimathea, being a disciple of Jesus, but secretly for fear of the Jews, besought Pilate that he might take away the body of Jesus: and Pilate gave him leave. He came therefore, and took the body of Jesus. And there came also Nicodemus, which at the first came by night and brought a mixture of myrrh and aloes, about an hundred pound weight. Then took they the body of Jesus, and wound it in linen clothes with the spices as the manner of the Jews is to bury." II Timothy 1:6-10 reads, "Wherefore I put you in remembrance that thou stir up the gift of God which is in thee by the putting on of my hands. For God hath not given us the spirit of fear but of power, and of love and of a sound mind. Be not thou therefore ashamed of the testimony of our Lord, nor of me His prisoner: but be thou partaker of the afflictions of the gospel according to the power of God; Who hath saved us, and called us with an holy calling, not according to our works but according to His own purpose and grace, which was given us in Christ Jesus before the world began. But is now made manifest by the appearing of Our Saviour Jesus Christ who hath abolished death, and hath brought life and immortality to light through the gospel:" and now John 20: 19. "Then the same day at evening being the first day of the week, when the doors were shut where the disciples were assembled for fear of the Jews came Jesus and stood in the midst and said unto them. Peace be unto you."

Notice that in all three of these scriptures we have followers or disciples of Jesus Christ. In all three scriptures fear of others and fear of reprisal kept them from witnessing for Jesus Christ and taking a stand for righteousness and standing against the enemy and the wiles of the devil. In the first scripture we have two disciples who when Jesus was alive on the earth were afraid to say much in standing with Him but now after death their love for Him causes them to put aside their fears to serve Jesus. In II Timothy Paul reminds Timothy that we have not been given the spirit of fear but instead God through Christ has given us the Spirit of power, love and a sound mind. That is the fact that we have been given the Holy Spirit who abides within and gives and leads us in power causing us to function in the agape love of God and leads us into all truth so that we understand all we have in Christ Jesus and we are not soon shaken in our minds that we should give in to fear. We are told that God saved us and called us with an holy calling according to His purpose and grace which was given to us before the world began in Christ Jesus. What a wonderful thought is it to know that redemption was also planned and that through the death and resurrection of our Saviour Jesus Christ, death has been abolished, and life and immortality is available for all mankind, who will believe and receive. Paul was saying to Timothy exactly what the word is saying to us. Don't be afraid of any man. Speak the truth in love. Preach the Gospel, endure the afflictions for Christ has overcome all and in Him we are over-comers. Then in the last scripture we just looked at fear had literally kept them bound unable to speak at all or even face the world who needed to hear. But remember on the day of Pentecost when they were all filled with the Holy Spirit they boldly spoke the wonderful things of God and when Peter preached the Gospel 3000+ were saved. Don't let fear rob you of what God has for you.

Exodus 1:15-20 reads, "And the king of Egypt spake to the Hebrew midwives, of which the name of the one was Shiphrah, and the name of the other Puah: And he said, when ye do the office of a midwife to the Hebrew women and see them upon the stools; if it be a son, then ye shall kill him; but if it be a daughter, then she shall live. But the midwives feared God, and did not as the king of Egypt commanded them but saved the men children alive. And the king of Egypt called for the midwives, and said unto them why have ye done this thing, and have saved the men children alive? And the midwives said unto Pharaoh, Because the Hebrew women are not as the Egyptian women: for they are lively, and are delivered ere that the midwives come in unto them. Therefore God dealt well with the midwives: and the people multiplied and waxed very mighty."

Did the midwives fear Pharaoh? The scripture doesn't say but I am quite sure they did, but their fear of the Lord was far greater than the fear of Pharaoh. And because of a godly fear of the living God they were protected and blessed.

In Romans 8:12-20 we read, "Therefore brethren, we are debtors, not to the flesh, to live after the flesh. For if ye live after the flesh, ye shall die: but if ye through the Spirit do mortify the deeds of the body, ye shall live. For as many as are led by the Spirit of God they are the sons of God. For ye have not received the spirit of bondage again to fear but ye have received the Spirit of adoption whereby we cry, Abba, Father. The Spirit itself beareth witness with our spirit that we are the children of God: and if children, then heirs of God and joint heirs with Christ; if so be that we suffer with Him, that we may be also glorified together. For I reckon that the sufferings of this present time are not worthy to be compared with the glory which shall be revealed in us. For the ernest expectation of the creature waiteth for the manifestation of the sons of God. For the creature was made subject to vanity, not willingly, but by reason of Him who hath subjected the same in hope."

Don't worry about the things of the flesh, don't return to bondage, don't give in to fear. The things we suffer in serving Christ are nothing in comparison to the glory we shall share with Him as joint heirs. We are God's children, we are the Kings kids if we have given our lives to Him and as we keep His commandments we abide in His love and are one with God, blessed eternally.

Look at first John 4:18. "There is no fear in love. but perfect love casteth out fear: because fear hath torment. He that feareth is not made perfect in love." Now if you are learning to abide in the Vine you know that you are told the following in John 15:7-10. "If ye abide in Me, and My words abide in you, ye shall ask what ye will and it shall be done Unto you. Herein is My Father glorified, that ye bear much fruit; so shall ye be My disciples. As the Father hath loved Me so have I loved you: continue ye in My love. If ye keep My commandments, ye shall abide in My love; even as I have kept My Father's commandments, and abide in His love." The abiding life in Jesus Christ brings such a depth of intimacy, as you are truly one with God, that fear can't exist and you become very fruitful in all you do and bring glory to the Father.

I want to look at two more portions of the Word of God before ending this chapter on Overcoming our Fears.

Hebrews 13:1-6 reads as follows, "Let brotherly love continue. Be not forgetful to entertain strangers: for thereby some have entertained angels unawares. Remember them that are in bonds, as bound with them; and them which suffer adversity as being yourselves also in the body. Marriage is honourable in all, and the bed undefiled: but whoremongers and adulterers God will judge. Let your conversation be without covetousness; and be content with such things as ye have: for He hath said I will never leave thee nor forsake thee. So that we may boldly say, The Lord is my helper and I will not fear what man shall do unto me."

As we continue through the river of life, love and serve man, be content with what you have and fear not.

The final scripture I want to look at is Psalm 27. "The Lord is my <u>light</u>, and my <u>salvation:</u> whom shall I fear? The Lord is the <u>strength</u> of <u>my life</u>: of whom shall I be afraid? When the wicked even mine enemies and my foes, come upon me to eat up my flesh, they stumbled and fell. Though an host should encamp against me, my <u>heart</u> shall <u>not fear</u>: though <u>war</u> should rise against me <u>in this will I be confident.</u> One thing have I desired of the Lord, that will I <u>seek</u> after; that I may <u>dwell in the house of the Lord</u> all the days of my life, to <u>behold</u> the beauty of <u>the Lord</u>, and to <u>enquire</u> in His Temple. For in the time of trouble <u>He shall hide me</u> in <u>His pavilion:</u> in the secret of <u>His tabernacle</u> shall He hide me; He shall <u>set me upon a rock,</u> and now shall mine head be lifted up above mine enemies round about me; therefore will <u>I offer in His tabernacle sacrifices of joy:</u> I will <u>sing,</u> yea, I will <u>sing praises</u> unto the Lord. Hear, O Lord, when I cry with my voice<u>: have mercy</u> also upon me and answer me. When Thou saidst Seek ye my face: my heart said unto Thee, <u>Thy face Lord, will I seek</u>. Hide not thy face far from me: put not Thy servant away in anger: <u>Thou</u> hast been <u>my help</u>; leave me not. neither forsake me, the Lord will take me up. <u>Teach me Thy way,</u> O Lord, and <u>lead</u> me in a plain path, because of mine enemies. <u>Deliver me</u> <u>not over unto the will of mine enemies:</u> for false witnesses are risen up against me, and such as breathe out cruelty. <u>I had fainted, unless I had believed</u> to see the goodness of the Lord in the land of the living. Wait on the Lord: be of good courage, and <u>He shall strengthen thine heart. Wait I say on the Lord."</u>

David knew problems and he knew enemies and yet he knew how to overcome fear, who to turn to, and trust in.

He also knew that He would fear and even faint for fear if he didn't know and understand and believe and trust in the goodness of the Lord.

If you and I react, as did David, we can overcome all fear. The Lord is our light to guide our path along the way. He is our salvation and provides strength for our lives. He will fight for us, and if enemies, or our fears, surround us we can be assured that our hearts need not fail us for fear. If we seek to dwell in His presence, abide in Him, as He is in us, [for we are His temple], when trouble comes He is with us. And He will hide us. He has set us upon a rock. That rock is Christ Jesus and we are built upon that foundation which is Christ. He is the Chief corner stone and we as lively stones are set upon Him. Victory is ours in that intimate relationship. We are His temple, and as we bring sacrifices of joy from within and sing praises unto the Lord, we know He hears and His mercies are new every morning. As we seek the Lord with our whole heart we can trust in His help knowing that He will never leave us nor forsake up. As we study to show ourselves approved and learn His ways and allow Him to lead us in His plain path we will know his deliverance and protection. We don't need to faint or give in to any fear that comes at us. Instead, as we seek Him, trust in Him, believe in His goodness, wait upon Him and be of good courage we will find that He will strengthen our hearts. We will also discover that fear will cease. We will overcome all fears, be filled with all joy and make it through every difficult time we face as we race to the finish line.

Chapter X
"A True Disciple And Yielded Servant"
(The Way Up Is Down)

As we look at what it means to be a true disciple the one thing we need to remember first and foremost is that a disciple never becomes greater than his master but is daily becoming like his master. In the case of becoming a disciple of Jesus Christ, that is one tall order but it is what we are to attain unto. Paul says in Philippians 3:7-14, "But what things were gain to me those I counted loss for Christ. Yea doubtless, and I count all things but loss for the excellency of the knowledge of Christ Jesus my Lord: for whom I have suffered the loss of all things, and do count them but dung, that I may win Christ. And be found in Him not having mine own righteousness which is of the law but that which is through the faith of Christ, the righteousness which is of God by faith: That I may know Him and the power of His resurrection, and the fellowship of His sufferings, being made conformable unto His death; If by any means I might attain unto the resurrection of the dead. Not as though I had already attained, either were already perfect: but I follow after, if that I may apprehend, that for which also I am apprehended of Christ Jesus. Brethren I count not myself to have apprehended: but this one thing I do, forgetting those things which are behind, and reaching forth unto those things which are before. I press toward the mark for the prize of the high calling of God in Christ Jesus."

Paul understood that everything he sought or pursued for himself and his own purposes, instead of drawing him into an intimate relationship with Jesus Christ and giving him a greater understanding of the Master, was separating him from becoming as his Master. Because of all he thought he was gaining was in reality loss. Paul had come to understand that in order to become like Christ requires that one must know Him intimately through faith and becoming conformed unto His death and know the power of His resurrection and the fellowship of His sufferings. Through this we might attain unto the resurrection of the dead. Paul also understood that being a true disciple and becoming like our Lord was not something that happens overnight. He knew he had not fully apprehended or attained the result he was seeking, but he wouldn't look back. Instead he reached forth for what was ahead and pressed toward that high mark which was the prize of the high calling of God in Christ Jesus.

In order to become like Christ it requires a mind set of being dead to self and only becoming like our Lord. It means we never look back and are always striving to know Him so we can be like Him.

A disciple is much more than simply a follower of a teacher. Instead he is one who learns or understands. To learn means to gain or acquire information or knowledge by instruction, through study, observation or experience; and to understand means to apprehend or comprehend fully the meaning of that which you have been taught. A true disciple listens to the lesson being taught, studies the lesson or application of the lesson and observes the teacher in His application of the lesson being taught. He then meditates upon the lesson and applies and practices the lesson so that the truth of what is being taught is fully understood and becomes a part of the disciple as it was of the master.

The second thing is this: The word disciple and the word discipline come from the same root word. In Greek the word is [mateo], which means to learn and understand and from which the word mathematics comes which carries the connotation of precise and accurate. The Hebrew word is [muwear], from which we get the meanings warning, instruction, reproof, chastening, chastisement, rebuke, doctrine and discipline. So we need to see that a true disciple is one who is disciplined in the things of the teacher or who has learned to yield to the hand or voice of correction and accept reproof and chastening when it is given by the teacher to cause you to learn and understand the lessons being taught. Until we reach this point in our following of Christ we cannot fully refer to ourselves as disciples of Jesus Christ.

The third thing is this. A disciple is only a disciple as long as he is either becoming like his master or teacher who is discipling him. If he becomes greater or above his teacher or master he ceases to be a disciple for he is no longer learning from him. Of course we know that in the case of being Jesus disciples we can never become greater than He, for He is God.

In order for one to make disciples of all nations it requires two things:
1) We must become true disciples of Jesus Christ and become like Him.
2) We must not teach man's interpretation of God's word, but instead teach fully the Word of God.

As we look at becoming a true disciple or a yielded servant we must first realize that to become a disciple of Jesus Christ is to obtain the pinnacle of the high calling and it is truly seeking to become great or to become all we are created to be for as we grow in the abiding relationship with our Lord we are changed from glory to glory as we become like Him. As we pursue this goal we must first understand that we have to be free from pride and second that we must humble ourselves under the mighty hand of God. No matter how we look at it we can never become like Christ until we realize that the way up is indeed down.

Matthew 18:3-4 reads, ".......... Verily I say unto you Except ye be converted and become as little children, ye shall not enter into the Kingdom of heaven. Whosoever therefore shall humble himself as this little child the same is greatest in the kingdom of heaven." and Matthew 23:8-12 says, "But be not ye called Rabbi: for one is your Master even Christ: and all ye are brethren. And call no man your father upon the earth: for one is your Father, which is in heaven. Neither be ye called masters for one is your Master, even Christ. But he that is greatest among you shall be your servant. And whosoever shall exalt himself shall be abased and he that shall humble himself shall be exalted." Philippians 2:5-11 reads, Let this mind be in you, which was also in Christ Jesus: Who being in the form of God, thought it not robbery to be equal with God: But made Himself of no reputation, and took upon Him the form of a servant and was made in the likeness of men: and being found in fashion as a man, He humbled Himself, and became obedient unto death, even the death of the cross. Wherefore God also hath highly exalted Him, and given Him a name which is above every name. That at the name of Jesus every knee should bow, of things in heaven and things in earth, and things under the earth; and that every tongue should confess that Jesus Christ is Lord, to the glory of God the Father."

To become like Christ requires that we are dead to self, that we don't think of ourselves more highly than we should and that we have crucified the old nature and are alive only in and through the resurrection life of Jesus Christ. The desire to be like and attain unto our Master [Jesus Christ], is God given and should vibrate in every cell of our bodies. The desire for Greatness is given you by God. "But Jesus called them to Him, and said unto them, Ye know that they which are accounted to rule over the Gentiles exercise authority upon them. But so shall it not be among you: but whosoever will be great among you shall be your minister: And whomsoever of you will be chiefest, shall be servant of all. For even the Son of man came not to be ministered unto but to minister and to give His life a ransom for many." [Mark 10:42-45]. Yes the desire for greatness was placed in you by God and His purpose is that you would be like your Master, your teacher, your leader, your Lord [Jesus Christ] and it all begins with humility. In order for us to become legitimate true disciples of Christ there is much about our lives that have to change so never forget, **The Way Up is Down!**

Let's take a moment to look back at the life of Paul as an example of a true disciple. In the beginning Paul was a disciple of Gamaliel. Now Gamaliel was a Pharisee and according to Jewish history one of the foremost teachers of Hebrew law at that time. Paul had been raised under his tutelage and had sat at his feet becoming like him and very zealous for the ways of God as he understood them even to the point of persecuting the church for he saw it as heresy as far as he understood scripture. Paul had become a real disciple of Gamaliel as the scripture says, he was 'a Pharisee of Pharisees'.

But praise God there came a day when Paul met the true and living Lord on the road to Damascus and as his spiritual eyes were opened he ceased to be a disciple of Gamaliel for he truly understood more than his teacher and at that point he became a disciple of Jesus Christ. From that point on his desire was to fully know and understand his master through fellowshipping with every aspect of Christ's life, sufferings, death and resurrection. He was not concerned with what he must suffer for the Lord. He was only concerned with becoming like his Lord and attaining unto the ultimate in that heavenly goal.

Is that your desire? If it is it will require all you are and all you have. If not you will fall short of reaching that goal that our Lord has placed in front of you and prepared you for. I don't mean you will miss heaven but it is God's desire that you become a true disciple and a yielded servant doing your job as a living stone in the house of God furthering the goal of taking the 'Good News' to the whole world that the glory of God would reach the ends of the earth and that you are truly changed from glory to glory into the image of His Son.

Paul said, "Follow me as I follow Christ." Never did Paul say become my disciple. Christ is our only Master. we are to become like Him.

Let's look at a number of scriptures and see where we stand as disciples of our Lord. I suggest that you take an honest accounting of your life, as I am, and make any changes that need to be made in order to obtain the goal of reaching, "the prize of the high calling of God in Christ Jesus."

Matthew 10:16-28 reads, "behold, I send you forth as sheep in the midst of wolves: be ye therefore wise as serpents, and harmless as doves. But beware of man: for they will scourge you in their synagogues; And ye shall be brought before governors and kings for My sake, for a testimony against them and the Gentiles. But when they deliver you up, take no thought how or what ye shall speak: for it shall be given you in that same hour what ye shall speak. For it is not you that speak, but the Spirit of your Father which speaketh in you. And the brother shall deliver up the brother to death, and the father the child: and the children shall rise up against their parents, and cause them to be put to death. And ye shall be hated of all men for my name's sake; but he that endureth to the end shall be saved. But when they persecute you in this city, flee ye into another: for verily I say unto you. Ye shall not have gone over the cities of Israel, till the Son of man be come. The disciple is not above his master, nor the servant above his lord. If they have called the Master of the house Beelzebub, how much more shall they call them of His household? Fear them not therefore for there is nothing covered that shall not be revealed: and hid that shall not be known. What I tell you in darkness, that speak in light: and what ye hear in the ear, that preach ye upon the housetops. And fear not them which kill the body, but are not able to kill the soul: but rather fear Him which is able to destroy both soul and body in hell."

Remember from our study of facing our fears that there is a healthy fear and that is the fear of the Lord. All other fear should cease as we grow into the likeness of Christ and become like Him for perfect love casts out fear. If we will become like Christ then we need to realize that we will be treated with the same scorn and hatred as He was and even if we face death we must endure to the end for it is as we endure that we will be saved. We can not give up short of the finish line. The rewards and crowns that await us and the inheritance that is ours and the promise of ruling and reigning with Christ Jesus require that we suffer with Him. Do you have a mind to suffer? I don't mean do you go out of your way to suffer or seek to be a martyr but do you fully identify with Christ's sufferings and count yourself blessed when you face persecution for your stand as a child of God and disciple of Christ. If that is you then you are moving one step closer to becoming a true disciple of Jesus, your Lord.

Luke 9:23-26 reads, "And He said to them all, if any man will come after Me, let him deny himself, and take up his cross daily, and follow me. For whosoever will lose his life for My sake, the same shall save it. For what is a man advantaged, if he gain the whole world, and lose himself, or be cast away? For whosoever shall be ashamed of Me and of My words, of him shall the Son of man be ashamed, when He shall come in His own Glory, and in His Father's and the holy angel's."

Being a true disciple requires that we die to our own purposes and desires for achievement and recognition in this world and daily take up that cross, that burden, [whatever it is that Christ has given you to bear], and fully or completely follow Him every day of your life. There are no vacation days. You have been bought with a price. That price is the precious shed blood of Jesus Christ. As such you are not your own but your life belongs to the Lord. As the temple of the living God your life is to be lived for Him as daily you live and walk in the Spirit. One thing we need to always remember is that the cross we bear or the yoke we carry or burden we now carry is that which our Lord has given and we don't bear it alone. He says of that burden, "Take My yoke upon you, and learn of Me; for I am meek and lowly in heart: and ye shall find rest unto your souls. For My yoke is easy and My burden is light." [Matthew 11:29-30}.

As we are joined together as one in Christ, if we should ever feel that the burden or cross we must carry is too much for us, we need simply remember that it isChrist who bore all our sins and the weight of them upon Himself on the cross to redeem us and to give us eternal life and the cross we now bear, our risen Saviour now bears with us as we daily walk with Him in intimate fellowship as His disciples.

Matthew 19:16-24 reads, "And behold, one came and said unto Him, Good Master, what good thing shall I do, that I may have eternal life? And He said unto him, Why callest thou Me good? there is none good but one, that is God: but if thou will enter into life, keep the commandments. He saith unto Him, Which? Jesus said, Thou shalt do no murder, Thou shalt not commit adultery. Thou shalt not steal. Thou shalt not bear false witness, Honour thy father and thy mother; and Thou shalt love thy neighbor as thyself. The young man saith unto Him, all these things have I kept from my youth up: what lack I yet? Jesus saith unto him, If thou wilt be perfect, go and sell that thou hast, and give to the poor, and thou shalt have treasure in heaven: and come and follow Me. But when the young man heard that saying, he went away sorrowful: for he had great possessions. Then said Jesus unto His disciples, Verily I say unto you, that a rich man shall hardly enter into the kingdom of heaven. and again I say unto you, It is easier for a camel to go through the eye of a needle, than for a rich man to enter into the kingdom of God."

Riches can be a great blessing in providing for the furthering of the purposes of the Kingdom of God or they can become a great snare to many preventing them from entering into the kingdom of God. "No man can serve two masters: for either he will hate the one, and love the other; or else he will hold to the one and despise the other. Ye cannot serve God and mammon." [Matthew 6:24]. It is not easy to forsake all to follow Christ and yet that is the mark of a true disciple.

Luke 9:57-62 says, "And it came to pass, that, as they went in the way, a certain man said unto Him, Lord, I will follow thee whithersoever Thou goest. And Jesus said unto him, Foxes have holes, and birds of the air have nests; but the Son of Man hath not where to lay His head. And he said unto another follow Me. But he said, Lord, suffer me first to go bury my father. Jesus said unto him, Let the dead bury their dead: but go thou and preach the kingdom of God. And another also said, Lord, I will follow thee; but let me first go bid them farewell, which are at home at my house. And Jesus said unto him, No man having put his hand to the plough, and looking back is fit for the kingdom of God."

As we take a close look at each of these scriptures we will come to understand what becoming a complete disciple and true follower of our Lord entails and come to understand the price of discipleship. In the first instance we need to understand that the normal comforts of life are not promised. There will be times that we will lack even a place to lay our heads for sleep, so if sleep and comfort are something you cannot do without you will find it very hard to fully follow and fulfill all the Lord has for you to do as His disciple. He does not want you to fall short of the goal but He does want you to understand the cost.

In the case of the second person that the Lord told to follow Him who asked to first go bury his father, our Lord's response was very clear and at first glance might seem harsh but really wasn't. It doesn't matter whether the man's father was at the point of death or could live many years, the point is to become a disciple is to become like the Master and Jesus had left all including His place in heaven with the Father to come and give His life on the cross to redeem all who would come unto Him unto eternal life and He has given us the commandment to go into all the world and preach the Gospel thereby continuing to fulfill the purpose of redemption. The moment Jesus began to preach He preached that the kingdom of God was at hand and we are commanded to do the same. In the final case Jesus response to the one who said I will follow you Lord 'but let me bid farewell to those at home first', shows that it wasn't simply saying good-by and leaving that was the point, it was the timing. This can be looked at in several ways, Number one is that the man was referring to still having children at home and once grown and gone then he would follow. The second possibility was that he would go and say good-by and at a convenient time he would return and follow the Lord. And you can put your own spin on it. No matter how you look at the man, Jesus fully understood him and drew a very vivid picture.

If you have ever watched a person plow with a team of oxen or horses, or if you yourself have ever done that then you understand the concept of looking back. First of all we must remember that the road to heaven is straight and narrow. Now imagine controlling a team of oxen while walking behind it with the plow and looking back at where you have been. You will very quickly lose your direction and no longer continue on the straight path. When you reach the other side of the field, [provided you reach the other side], you will have plowed a path that looks like a snake and be in need of doing it all over again. Once we start to follow the leading of our Lord we must never take our eyes off the goal of becoming like our Master and finishing the race set before us. Can you imagine the disaster you would have if while riding a river-board, instead of looking at the rapids ahead of you, you turn to watch the rapids you just left? Wipeout!

In Luke 14:26-27 we read, "If any man come to me, and hate not his father, and mother, and wife, and children, and brethren, and sisters, yea and his own life also, he cannot be My disciple." At first glance, looking at this scripture it seems incongruous that the Lord would tell us that in order to follow Him we must hate those closest to us when God is love and we are told to even love our enemies and that the world will know we are His disciples by the love we have one for another. But when you understand the application of the word translated hate, which is the Greek word [miseo] which comes from the primary word [misos] or hatred: to detest or to persecute and realize the extended meaning of [miseo] is to love less in relationship to your love of the Lord it is easy to understand for there is no comparison. So if you were to draw a thermometer, love for self and others would be at the very bottom and love for the Lord would be off the top. It is not a question of hate Vs love but instead a question of putting Christ far above our love for anything or anyone. Then in the second part of the scripture where it refers to bearing our cross we need to see this; The word bear is the Greek word [bastazo] from the base word [basace] a pace, and means literally [endure, declare, sustain, receive]. So bearing or taking up our cross means to receive the cross we are given, willingly declaring it unto the world and enduring whatever it takes as we commit to becoming like Christ, entering into the abiding relationship as His true disciples. And if we relate to all the meaning here of the cross from the word [stauros], literally a pole or cross as an instrument of capital punishment and figuratively exposure to death, self denial and identify in the atonement of Christ. In other words we must daily deny self, facing exposure to death and willingly declare the meaning of Christ's death upon the cross as the atonement for sin. If we don't openly profess and proclaim His death and resurrection to the world each and every day we are not entering into the abiding relationship we were created for and are not worthy of becoming His disciples. Becoming like our Lord is not a cake walk. It requires commitment and guts.

John 13:16 reads, "Verily, verily, I say unto you, the servant is not greater than his lord; neither he that is sent greater that he that sent him." When Jesus spoke these words he had just risen from the table and taken a towel and a pitcher and basin of water and washed the disciples feet. Once more He had taken the position of a servant and yet He was and is the Master, Lord and God. Always remember it is Jesus we are to follow and strive hard after to become like. Are you serving man or your own wants and desires? Where do you stand on becoming like Christ? John 13:34-35 says, "A new commandment I give unto you, that ye love one another; as I have loved you, that ye also love one another. By this shall all men know that ye are My disciples, if ye have love one to another."

All three times the word love and loved is used, it is the word [agapeo] which is the total unselfish all giving love of God. It is not enough to love in the human friendship love but instead the commandment which Jesus was here establishing, shortly before going to the cross, was based upon the totality of His love which was the motivating force that caused Him to leave heaven and come to the earth and His Creation, and give His all including His very life to become the redeemer as well as creator. He was saying unto His disciples,[and if you consider yourself His disciple, you as well], that they, and you and I must love unconditionally all mankind. It is that love that shows the world we are His disciples.

John 15:18-21 reads, "If the world hate you, ye know that it hated Me before it hated you. If ye were of the world, the world would love his own: but because ye are not of the world, but I have chosen you out of the world, therefore the world hateth you. Remember the word that I said unto you. The servant is not greater than his lord, If they have persecuted Me, then they will also persecute you; if they have kept My sayings, they will keep yours also. But all these things will they do unto you for My name's sake, because they know not Him that sent Me." II Thessalonians 2:13-14 reads, "But we are bound to give thanks always to God for you, brethren beloved of the Lord, because God hath from the beginning chosen you to salvation through the sanctification of the Spirit and belief of the truth; Wherefore He called you by our gospel, to the obtaining of the glory of our Lord Jesus Christ."

Both II Thessalonians and John tell us that we were chosen to come to salvation and sanctification through the Spirit and the belief in the truth of God's Word of Christ's atoning death upon the cross as our sacrifice. Christ died for all and those who choose to accept the free gift and choose to follow Him can expect to be hated by the world. If you find yourself being totally accepted by the world you need to ask yourself if you are really abiding in Christ and becoming all it means to be a disciple of the Master Himself.

We have read John 15:7-11 before and as Christ disciple you should be very familiar with it and if not open your

Bible and read it again. Evidence of our being true disciples comes as we keep His commandments and bring glory unto the Father through bearing much fruit which only comes through our abiding in the Lord and His Word abiding in us. It also assures us of a love relationship with the Son and the Father that will remain and a joy that is full as Christ's joy remains in us.

Let's shift gears slightly for a minute and look at John 19:26-27. "When Jesus therefore saw His mother, and the disciple standing by, whom He loved, He saith unto His mother, Woman behold thy son. Then saith He to the disciple, Behold thy mother: And from that hour that disciple took her unto his own home."

A true disciple sometimes may be asked by the Lord to take responsibility for something that may seem an added burden but be assured whatever you are called upon to do he will give you the ability and grace to fulfill.

Matthew 5:18 reads, "Be ye therefore perfect even as your Father which is in heaven is perfect." and II Timothy 3:16-17 says, "All scripture is given by inspiration of God and is profitable for doctrine, for reproof, for correction, for instruction in righteousness, that the man of God may be perfect, throughly furnished unto all good works."

In order to be a true disciple it requires that we become complete as our heavenly Father is complete and that completeness in part comes from our understanding of the word of God. As we learn to abide, maturity and completeness comes to our lives and we become more like our Saviour.

Before we leave this chapter on a true disciple and a yielded servant I want to look at one final scripture in the book of Acts, and we could take the entire book of Acts and study the lives of the followers of Christ who were true *disciples, but I simply wish to look at one and that is in Acts 11:25-26. "Then departed Barnabas to Tarsus for to seek Saul; And when he had found him, he brought him unto Antioch, And it came to pass, that a whole year they assembled themselves with the church and taught much people, and the disciples were called Christians first in Antioch." It is interesting that the word Christian or follower of Christ referred to disciples. **IF** you were required to be a true disciple in order to be called a Christian today, the number of Christians would be greatly reduced.*

Are you willing to forsake all, take up your cross daily, proclaim the truth and enter into the abiding relationship that moves you into the inner circle of a true disciple and causes you to continue to press toward the mark of the prize of the high calling of God in Christ jesus as you continue through the river of life toward the ultimate goal of finishing the Race and hearing the words, "Well done thou good and faithful servant."?

Chapter XI
"The Missed Gate"

In ski races, kayak races and some river-board races it is vital that you make a clear transition through every gate. A missed gate can cost you not only the loss of time but the loss of a race. As you and I maneuver the race course set before us in the river of life a missed gate can also cost us dearly, becoming a great setback and if not regaining our bearings and composure a missed gate can also knock us out of the race.

So you say, what do I mean by a missed gate. In a race on water, gates are set up where you must turn and fight your way against the current back up stream and move through a gate or around an obstacle and then continue on down stream toward the finish line. In a downhill ski race you are moving at break neck speeds as you move around poles in and through gates. Both take a great deal of strength and concentration as you strive to overcome the obstacles set in your path that you must conquer to reach the goal of winning the race. In the race of life there are times we must fight for all we are worth seemingly moving upstream against all obstacles to overcome the temptations hurled against us and there are times we seem to be moving at break neck speed toward the finish line easily moving in and out and through every gate overcoming every temptation hurled our way when just one small miscalculation can send us reeling and if not quickly regaining our balance find ourselves out of the race in great trouble. It is one thing to get blind sided or miss a gate and lose a physical race but it is quite a different thing to give into temptation in the race we find ourselves in, in the river of life, and find ourselves unable to rebound. As Jesus drew near to the completion of His earthly ministry He knew how difficult it was to be barraged by temptations as He had asked Peter, James and John to watch and pray with Him and quickly discovered that they had fallen asleep. He then said this to them. "Watch ye and pray, lest ye enter into temptation. The spirit truly is ready, but the flesh is weak." [Mark 14:38}. In the same way that your physical eyes must be open to even the slightest change so you never miss a gate: we must have our eyes wide open focussed on Christ and watching for any appearance of the enemy coming our way with an attempt to knock us off course. It is not enough to simply watch, we need to pray, As we are given to prayer and praying without ceasing our focus will be such that nothing will take us by surprise.

In the parable of the sower and soils as Jesus told in Luke 8:13 we read, "They on the rock are they, which when they hear, receive the word with joy: and these have no root, which for a while believe and in time of temptation fall away." On the surface you may think that you love the Lord and are growing in that relationship but life in Christ can't be a shallow thing. It requires a heart and life totally given over to Jesus. If you are not fully abiding in the Lord, when you face temptation, Jesus says you will fall away. If you abide in Him and His word abides in you, you will overcome each temptation that comes and never miss a gate or give in to sin. But we need to be aware that if we think we can stand against the wiles of the devil and overcome every test and temptation, successfully maneuvering through every gate, and never give in to sin on our own, we better think twice. Paul says this, as led by the Spirit of God to write it down, in I Corinthians 10:12-13, "Wherefore let him that think he standeth take heed lest he fall. There hath no temptation taken you but such as is common to man: but God is faithful, who will not suffer you to be tempted above that ye are able; but will with the temptation also make a way to escape, that ye may be able to bear it. Every gate or obstacle that you face, others have faced before you. It isn't something new that only you must face. There is a way around or through every test or temptation. You can conquer every gate. You must remain focused on the Lord. He makes the way. He is the way through every gate of temptation.

There is one gate that has destroyed and drowned many. Look at I Timothy 6:9-11. "But they that will be rich fall into temptation and a snare, and into many foolish and hurtful lists, which drown men in destruction and perdition. For the love of money is the root of all evil: which while some coveted after, they have erred from the faith, and pierced themselves through with many sorrows. But thou, O man of God, flee these things: and follow after righteousness, godliness, faith, love, patience, meekness."

Now you may say, 'I don't have any problem with money. I've never been rich. I barely have enough to get by." Just because you aren't rich doesn't mean you don't have the desire to be rich or have the desire to have the things riches can bring. It isn't having money that is the problem but the love of money and what it can provide that is the problem. You could be as poor as a church mouse or as rich as Bill Gates and maneuver through that gate just fine or desire what you don't have and lust after those things which can and will destroy you through unlawful gain [if poor] or misuse what you do have in desires for more, wrecking havoc. David said in Psalms 62:10,"Trust not in oppression, and become not vain in robbery: if riches increase, set not your heart upon them." and in Proverbs 30:7-9 it says, "Two things have I required of Thee, deny me them not before I die: Remove far from me vanity and lies: give me neither poverty nor riches, feed me with food convenient for me: Lest I be full and deny Thee, and say, Who is the Lord? or lest I be poor, and steal, and take the name of my God in vain."

Both Psalms and Proverbs make the point that acquiring or possessing of riches can turn your heart unto the riches themselves and away from God, godly desires and I Timothy told us that the very desire for riches can cause us to error from the faith and pierce ourselves through with many sorrows and drown us in destruction and perdition. Failing in that temptation and missing that gate can mean the difference between heaven and hell. God knows what each of us need and when it says in Proverbs, "feed me with food convenient for me" it is saying God give me what you prescribe. Both poverty and riches are impostors and can cause us to turn from God. Contentment is the victor over both and the way through that gate or temptation.

The last part of what we read in I Timothy said to flee the desires for riches and the lusts and sorrows that come with those desires and "follow after righteousness, godliness, faith, love, patience, meekness." If we fill our hearts with the things of God we will be spared the hurts that come from setting our hearts upon riches.

Unlike the gates in a race which man creates and places in position; **to test our skills; create our thrills, and cause our spills:** *the gates of temptations we face in the race of life are of our own doing provided by Satan and our lusts. They all allowed by God to perfect us so that when we endure and conquer the temptations and successfully make it through each gate we shall receive the crown of life.* **There may be thrills in the temptations you face and you may feel you can handle them but beware and take heed lest you fall. Don't take pride in your skill or ability to overcome the thrill and take a spill that can ultimately kill.** *James 1: 12-15 reads, "Blessed is the man that endureth temptation: for when he is tried, he shall receive the crown of life, which the Lord hath promised to them that love Him. Let no man say when he is tempted, I am tempted of God: for God cannot be tempted with evil, neither tempteth He any man: But every man is tempted, when he is drawn away of his own lust, and enticed. Then* *when lust hath conceived, it bringeth forth sin: and sin when it is finished, bringeth forth death."*

The temptations we face, God allows. How we handle each will determine whether we are successful in getting through the gate and growing thereby or failing. James 1:2-4 says, "My brethren, count it all joy when ye fall into divers temptations: Knowing this, that the trying of your faith worketh patience. But let patience have her perfect work, that ye may be perfect and entire, wanting nothing." In a natural race there is joy as well as a thrill as you face each gate and here James says we should count it all joy when we face temptation because like gates in a race, they are there for us to conquer, not be defeated by, and cause us to grow and mature. Remember the Lord doesn't let us face temptations alone. we will not be trapped or drowned by what we face. He promises to give us a way of escape or a way through. We simply need to stay focused [ON HIM]. He will deliver the godly out of temptations, in other words the temptation will not defeat the righteous and draw them into sin as long as they stay focused upon the Lord. II Peter 2:9 reads, "The Lord knoweth how to deliver the godly out of temptations, and to reserve the unjust unto the day o judgement to be punished:"

We need to remember we are not facing temptations that others have never faced and also that Jesus was tempted in all ways that you and I are tempted but He was without sin. Jesus has run the race ahead of us and conquered every gate and knows how to lead us through. So whether you are facing the gate marked "lust of the eyes", "lust of the flesh" or "pride of life", as you learn to abide in Christ, who has defeated Satan at every turn and overcome all temptations, you too will overcome all and be victorious. Jesus used the word to defeat Satan and we too can overcome by the use of the word of God as it abides in us.

If you see someone failing to make a gate in a race those who successfully make it usually give instruction to those who have failed so they make it the next time. But if you think you can handle everything and can ignore others you need to think twice. Look at Galatians 6:1-5. "Brethren, if a man be overtaken in a fault, ye which are spiritual restore such an one in the spirit of meekness considering thyself, lest thou also be tempted. Bear ye one another's burden; and so fulfill the law of Christ. For if a man think himself to be something when he is nothing, he deceiveth himself. But let every man prove his own work, and then shall he have rejoicing in himself alone, and not in another. For every man shall bear his own burden."

The race of life is unlike a physical race where there is a single winner and you are racing to be first against other contestants. In the river of life we are to help as many as we can reach the finish line and that requires that we bear one another's burdens and help others overcome temptations. At the same time it is our responsibility to humbly face every temptation bearing our own burden not trusting in ourselves but placing our trust fully in Christ. We need to remember that it is only through Christ that we can do all things. Outside of our relationship in Christ we are nothing and if you think otherwise you are deceiving yourself and allowing pride to rob you of the truth.

So what happens if we miss a gate and fail a temptation, give into sin, and find ourselves drowning and struggling to reach the surface? Is there hope? Is there a second chance? First of all let's look at the seriousness of a missed gate. In a physical race on water there is a great deal of physical energy that is expended to again fight upstream a second time after the initial attempt to make it through the gate. When strength is already weak this is a difficult process and second a great deal of time is lost that can cost you the race. In a ski race you don't have a second chance to make the gate but suffer a penalty which can also cost you the race. Now in the race of life which we find ourselves, a missed gate, which leads to sin, robs us of spiritual strength, penalizes us because of loss of effectiveness in our witness for Christ and causes us to have to fight through the same temptation all over again even if we do recover and find forgiveness. The loss of time can never be recovered and even if we finish the race in victory the work of the Lord suffers through our failure.

Our failure in missing a gate and succumbing to the temptation and falling into sin, separates us from God for He cannot look upon sin and the wages of sin is death. If we stop right there we would loose heart and have no hope of forgiveness and give up and drown in our sorrows. Isaiah 59:2 reads, "but your iniquities have separated between you and your God and your sins have hid His face from you, that He will not hear." So if that is the total picture, why fight back upstream having failed and fight through the temptation all over again and conquer the gate? Thank God that isn't the total picture. There is hope. There is a second chance and there is forgiveness. Look at the following scriptures and you will see that God doesn't give up on you. He has provided the way even when you have totally missed a gate and failed the test and feel lost and defeated. You can still gain an abiding relationship in and through Him who has conquered all, and become victorious. Isaiah 59:1, "Behold, the Lord's hand is not shortened, that it cannot save; neither His ear heavy, that it cannot hear:'. Isaiah 53:5 says, "But He was wounded for our transgressions, He was bruised for our iniquities: the chastisement of our peace was upon Him; and with His stripes we are healed.". Then in II Samuel 12:13 we read "And David said unto Nathan, I have sinned against the Lord. And Nathan said unto David, The Lord also hath put away thy sin; thou shalt not die.". II Chronicles 7:14 reads, "If My people, which are called by My name shall humble themselves, and pray, and seek My face, and turn from their wicked ways: then will I hear from heaven, and will forgive their sin, and will heal their land." Psalm 32:5 says this, "I acknowledge my sin unto thee, and mine iniquity have I not hid. I said, I will confess my transgressions unto the Lord; and Thou forgavest the iniquity of my sin. Selah." Romans 6:14, "For sin shall not have dominion over you: for ye are not under the law, but under grace." Romans 8:31-39, What shall we then say to these things? If God be for us, who can be against us? He that spared not His own Son but delivered Him up for us all, how shall He not with Him also freely give us all things? Who shall lay anything to the charge of God's elect? It is God that justifieth. Who is he that condemeth? It is Christ that died, yea rather, that is risen again, who is even at the right hand of God, who also maketh intercession for us. Who shall separate us from the love of Christ? shall tribulation, or distress, or persecution, or famine, or nakedness, or peril, or sword? As it is written, For thy sake we are killed all the day long: we are accounted as sheep for the slaughter. Nay in all these things we are more than conquerors through Him that loved us. For I am persuaded, that neither death, nor life, nor angels, nor principalities, nor powers nor things present, nor things to come, Nor height, nor depth, nor any other creature, shall be able to separate us from the love of God, which is in Christ Jesus our Lord.". Ezekiel 33:14-16 says, "Again when I say unto the wicked, Thou shalt surely die: if he turn from his sin, and do that which is lawful and right; If the wicked restore the pledge, give again that he had robbed, walk in the statutes of life, without committing iniquity: he shall surely live, he shall not die. None of his sins that he hath committed shall be mentioned unto him: he hath done that which is lawful and right: he shall surely live." John 1:29 says, "The next day John seeth Jesus coming unto him, and saith, Behold the Lamb of God, which taketh away the sin of the world.". I John 1:7-10 said, "But if we walk in the light, as He is in the light, we have fellowship one with another, and the blood of Jesus Christ His Son cleanseth us from all sin. If we say that we have no sin, we deceive ourselves, and the truth is not in us. If we confess our sins, He is faithful and just to forgive us our sins, and to cleanse us from all unrighteousness. If we say that we have not sinned we make Him a liar, and His Word is not in us."

There is not one outside of Christ that has gone through the 'Race of Life' who has never missed a gate and fallen into sin but our Lord is always there to help us regain what has been lost, forgive us and help us to overcome and fight against all odds to reenter the race and make it through the gate which had almost destroyed us.

God is in the business of restoring as He said to His People in the book of Joel. Joel 2:12-13 and 25 says, "Therefore also now, saith the Lord, turn ye even to Me with all your heart, and with fasting, and with weeping and with mourning: And rend your heart, and not your garment, and turn unto the Lord your God: for He is gracious and merciful, slow to anger, and of great kindness .... and I will restore to you the years that the locust hath eaten, the cankerworm, and the caterpiller, and the palmerworm, My great army which I sent among you."

If you find that you have missed a gate don't give up. Repent, return and face it head on. Victory is only a prayer away.

Chapter XII
"A Rapid Change"

When you are in white water don't ever think you understand the river no matter how many times you have run races on the same stretch of river for water is so unpredictable and even a single rapid can change from the time you have gone through it and the person behind you enters it. A rapid, change can be a rapid change, or visa versa. If you have to think about what I just said for very long you had better stay out of the water.

But let's get back to the race we find ourselves in as we strive for perfection and 'press toward the mark for the prize of the high calling of God in Christ Jesus'. Things may be smooth one day and you are moving along with everything under control, blue sky above, your route and future set before you, security all around you. You are floating along relaxed and happy with not a care in the world when suddenly out of nowhere your smooth water becomes a torrent as a rapid change like a tornado destroys your tranquility, takes away the blue sky and leaves you all alone gasping for air. What do you do now? Can you recover? You had done everything right. You had committed your way unto the Lord. How could this have happened? How could God allow you to lose everything you held dear. You had put Him first before all else. You cry out in despair, "God Why?" As you fight for some answer you find yourself tossed over and over in the rapids. Where will it end and how will it end? Nothing but questions and seemingly no answers. One moment all is right and in the next moment all is wrong.

A rapid change can come to any of us at any time. It might come in the form of a death of a spouse, a parent, a child, a lover or friend. It could come as a loss of a job, an injury, robbery or bankruptcy. Or it could come in the form of a catastrophic event such as a tornado, a hurricane, a tsunami, or flood or fire. It could come as a mental breakdown, dementia, cancer or stroke. Maybe divorce or a combination of many different things can strike you at once. Wherever it comes from and in whatever form, the rapid change, can wreck havoc upon any who are not firmly abiding in Christ. Even Job, as he was struck with rapid change after rapid change, loosing all his children, servants, earthly goods and his health wanted answers and cried out for relief. However he never blamed God. What does it take to face rapid change and still maintain your integrity, and your trust in the Lord? When your faith is tested beyond measure can you remain steadfast and content? When the storms rage around you are you capable of having peace inside and finally when it seems that all hope is gone can you hang on hoping against hope and overcome?

As we find answers we need to remember that walking in righteousness does not exempt us from trouble. As Jesus instructed the disciples, [which is instruction for us as well], to treat everyone the same; with love, He made this statement in Matthew 5:45, "That ye may be the children of your Father which is in heaven: for He maketh His Son to rise on the evil and on the good, and tendeth rain on the just and the unjust." God treats all men the same, with His love and provision. He makes no difference in His love for all His creation. However, because sin entered into the world, because of the fall, Satan will do everything in his power to destroy both the just and the unjust. Because of this bad things do happen to good people. As we saw in the last chapter, how we respond determines how those things affect our lives. We are told in Romans 8:28-29, "And we know that all things work together for good to them that love God, to them who are the called according to His purpose. For whom He did foreknow, He also did predestinate to be conformed to the image of His Son that He might be the firstborn among many brethren." And we are also told in Romans 8:12-18 this, "Therefore, brethren, we are debtors, not to the flesh, to live after the flesh. For if ye live after the flesh, ye shall die: but if ye through the Spirit do mortify the deeds of the body, ye shall live. For as many as are led by the Spirit of God, They are the sons of God. For ye have not received the spirit of bondage again to fear: but ye have received the Spirit of adoption, whereby we cry, Abba Father. The Spirit itself beareth witness with our spirit, that we are the children of God, and joint-heirs with Christ; if so be that we suffer with Him, that we may be also glorified together. For I reckon that the sufferings of this present time are not worthy to be compared with the glory which shall be revealed in us." We looked at this scripture in chapter 9 in reference to facing your fears but it is good here for our study of Rapid Change to look at it again.

Persecution, problems and tribulations come to the just. It should be no surprise. Paul in writing to the Thessalonians in I Thessalonians 2:18 said, "Wherefore we would have come unto you, even I Paul once and again; but Satan hindered us." and inI Thessalonians 3:4, "For verily, when we were with you, we told you before that we should suffer tribulation; even as it came to pass, and ye know." Again we read in II Timothy 2:10-12, "Therefore I endure all things for the elect's sake, that they may also obtain the salvation which is in Christ Jesus with eternal glory. It is a faithful saying: For if we be dead with Him, we shall also live with Him; If we suffer, we shall also reign with Him: if we deny Him, He also will deny us:" Paul understood and wanted others to understand that even though the sufferings of this world were not of God, that they would come upon us, but God would use them to perfect us that we might be glorified with the Son. Paul was not taken by surprise for the Lord had told him how much he would suffer for Christ and you and I should not be taken unawares either. If we suffer for righteousness sake we are blessed but if our suffering is of our own doing there is only loss. Jesus said in Acts 9:16 in regards to Paul, "For I will shew him how great things he must suffer for My name's sake." And Paul tells us in Philippians 1:29, "For unto you it is given in the behalf of Christ, not only to believe on Him but also to suffer for His sake." Don't forget that all things work together for good to them that love God and are the called according to His purpose. Yes bad things do come to good people and how we respond will determine the extent of the good that comes from the rapid changes that come to rob us and destroy and cause suffering. Paul shows in Philippians 4:12-13 that the sudden difficulties, loses, hurts and pains that come your way don't need to destroy you. He said, "I know both how to be abased, and how to abound; everywhere and in all things I am instructed both to be full and to be hungry, both to abound and to suffer need. I can do all things through Christ which strengtheneth me," It is only through developing a deep abiding relationship in Christ that we can withstand the on-slot that can take us unaware at any time.

Let's look at other examples in the word of God and see if we can't learn from them, that when we are met with rapid change, and we find ourselves crying out to God, we can maintain our integrity, trusting in Him, standing in faith, peaceful and content, and overcome all things.

I want to begin to do this by looking at four scriptures from the book of Job and see what it says about Job maintaining his integrity through all of his sufferings, as rapid as they struck, and as devastating as they were.

In Job in the first chapter Satan is given permission to bring evil against Job as Satan challenged God and the conversation is recorded thus. Job 1:8-12 says, "And the Lord said unto Satan, Hast thou considered my servant job, that there is none like him in the earth, a perfect and an upright man, one that feareth God, and eschewed evil? Then Satan answered the Lord, and said, Doth Job fear God for nought? Hast not thou made an hedge about him, and about his house, and about all that he hath on every side? Thou hast blessed the work of his hands, and his substance is increased in the land. But put forth thine hand now, and touch all that he hath, and he will curse Thee to Thy face. And the Lord said unto Satan, Behold, all that he hath is in thy power; only upon himself put not forth thy hand. So Satan went forth from the presence of the Lord." In the rest of chapter one we see his servants killed, his live stock destroyed, all his possessions taken and his children dead. And yes he suffered greatly and even lost his children. Now be assured that God did not cause it, but yes He did allow it. You may ask how can one recover from such a loss especially the loss of all your children? How can anything good come from this? Well if you read the end of the book of Job you discover that Job in the end did come forth as gold. But you say what about his children? If you read carefully you will see that God blessed Job with twice as much as he had in the beginning but only gave him as many children as he had in the beginning. Now since God's Word cannot lie, when it says in Job 42:10, "And the Lord turned the captivity of Job, when he prayed for his friends: also the Lord gave Job twice as much as he had before." We can be assured that the children he lost to physical death were reunited with him in heaven.

Job suffered and mourned the loss of all and in Job 1:20-22 we read, "Then Job arose and rent his mantle, and shaved his head, and fell down upon the ground, and worshipped, and said, Naked came I out of my mothers womb, and naked shall I return thither: the Lord gave, and the Lord hath taken away; blessed be the name of the Lord. In all this Job sinned not nor charged God foolishly." Then again Satan comes before God and we read in Job 2:3-6, "And the Lord said unto Satan, Hast thou considered my servant Job, that there is none like him in the earth, a perfect and an upright man one that feareth God and escheweth evil? and still he holdeth fast his integrity, although thou movest me against him, to destroy him without a cause. And Satan answered the Lord, and said, skin for skin, yea, all that a man hath will he give for his life. But put forth Thine hand now, and he will curse Thee to Thy face. And the Lord said unto Satan, behold , he is in thine hand; but save his life." The suffering Job underwent was for the benefit of all who followed which includes us. Remember the suffering we endure is for Christ's sake and for the furthering of the Gospel. As we endure and maintain our integrity and trust in God as did Job; God's glory is revealed through His children. So another rapid, hits Job and he is covered with boils from the soles of his feet to the crown of his head and all that follows in the days to come bring no comfort or relief. Even his wife turns against him as we read in Job 2:9-10. "Then said his wife unto him, Dost thou still retain thine integrity? Curse God, and die. But he said unto her, Thou speakest as one of the foolish women speaketh. What? shall we receive good at the hand of God, and shall we not receive evil? In all this did not Job sin with his lips." As Job's friends accuse him instead of comforting , over and over in the coming days, Job refuses to agree with them and say they are right. Instead he maintains his stand and neither blames God nor accepts the blame himself. He instead determines to maintain his integrity. Look at Job26:6-27:6. "Hell is naked before Him, and destruction hath no covering. He stretcheth out the north over the empty place, and hangeth the earth upon nothing. He bindeth up the waters in his thick clouds; and the cloud is not rent under them. He holdeth back the face of His throne, and spreadeth His cloud upon it. He hath compassed the waters with bounds, until the day and night come to an end. The pillars of heaven tremble and as astonished at His reproof. He divideth the sea with His power, and by His understanding He smiteth through the proud. By His Spirit He hath garnished the heavens; His hand hath formed the crooked serpent. Lo, these are parts of His ways: but how little a portion is heard of Him? but the thunder of His power who can understand? Moreover Job continued his parable, and said , as God liveth, who hath taken away my judgement; and the Almighty, who hath visited my soul; all the while my breath is in me, and the spirit of God is in my nostrils; My lips shall not speak wickedness, nor my tongue utter deceit. God forbid that I should justify you: till I die I will not remove mine integrity from me."

Job knew God was the source of all and it was God who gave him life and only God who could take it or allow it to be taken from him. But in no way would he accuse God or admit to a lie as long as the breath of God was in his nostrils. In chapter 31 Job declares his innocence of the things his friends are accusing him, not in a prideful way, but simply stating the facts. He says he was innocent of sensual sins; of abusing his power, of trusting in his wealth and not being concerned for his enemies. In Job 31:5-6 we read, "If I have walked with vanity, or if my foot hath hasted to deceit: let me be weighed in an even balance, that God may know mine integrity." Job was staking everything upon his abiding relationship with the Lord. If we go back to the very first verse of the book of Job we read this in Job 1:1, "There was a man in the land of Uz, whose name was Job; and that man was perfect and upright and one that feared God and eschewed evil." And verse 5, "And it was so, when the days of their fasting were gone about, that Job sent and sanctified them, and rose up early in the morning, and offered burnt offerings according to the number of them all: for Job said, It may be that my sons have sinned and cursed God in their hearts. This did Job continually." Job had an ongoing intimate relationship with the Lord and he knew who he was in the Lord and through it all he maintained his integrity, trust, faith and peace accepting all that came his way.

In Psalm 25:15-21 we see this, "Mine eyes are ever toward the Lord: for He shall pluck my feet out of the net. Turn Thee unto me, and have mercy upon me; for I am desolate and afflicted. The troubles of my heart are enlarged: O bring Thou me out of my distresses. Look upon mine affliction and my pain; and forgive all my sins. Consider mine enemies, for they are many; and they hate me with a cruel hatred. O keep my soul and deliver me: let me not be ashamed; for I put my trust in Thee. Let integrity and uprightness preserve me: for I wait on Thee."

David knew no matter how great his affliction, that as long as he kept his eyes upon the Lord, placed his trust in Him and maintained that relationship, that the integrity and righteousness of the Lord would preserve him. We must always remember that our righteousness is as filthy rags and our integrity as nothing. It is only through the integrity and righteousness of the Lord that we are kept from total destruction. Notice in Psalm 26:1 David says, "Judge me, O Lord; for I have walked in mine integrity; I have trusted also in the Lord; therefore I shall not slide." No, David, like Job, was not boasting in his own ability but was referring to his trust and relationship in the Lord. It is our right standing with the Lord that we can walk in our own integrity. It is not in pride in ourselves or what we have done or accomplished. Psalm 41:12 says, "And as for me, Thou upholdest me in mine integrity, and settest me before Thy face for ever." Only God can keep us in our integrity. We must always trust and abide in order to remain before Him. Psalm 78:72 reads, "So He fed them according to the integrity of His heart; and guided them by the skillfulness of

His hands." *If we understand the goodness and greatness of the Lord and strive to be like Him we too at all times and in all circumstances will be able to maintain and walk and relate in the integrity of our hearts.*

Solomon also understood the vital importance of maintaining a life of integrity for he wrote in Proverbs 11:3, "The integrity of the upright shall guide them: but the perverseness of transgressors shall destroy them." And in Proverbs 19:1 he wrote, "Better is the poor that walketh in his integrity, than he that is perverse in his lips and is a fool." Solomon says that if you have nothing, [or let's say you have lost all] and still maintain your integrity you are much better off than one who is a lying fool or as Solomon put it in Proverbs 28:6, "Better is the poor that walketh in his uprightness, than he that is perverse in his ways though he be rich."

Maintaining our integrity, when everything is coming apart and we feel we are drowning in destruction can only exist as we abide in Christ and fully place our trust in Him. II Samuel 22:31 tells us, "As for God, His way is perfect; the word of the Lord is tried: He is a buckler to all them that trust in Him." David knew the importance of fully trusting in God and had learned to trust Him through many tests, trials, afflictions,and suffering and sorrows and in his darkest hours he always sought refuge in God. Job 13:15 says, "Though He slay me yet will I trust Him: but I will maintain my own ways before Him." Whether Job understood what God was allowing or why made no difference. He would walk before Him and place his trust in the Lord. Then in Psalm 20:7 David emphatically makes the point that trust only belongs in God. "Some trust in chariots and some in horses; but we will remember the name of the Lord our God." In the 49th Psalm David shows the futility of placing your trust in riches. and this is even more evident when sudden or rapid changes come that bring loss and sorrow to your life. Psalm 49:5-17 reads, "Wherefore should I fear in the days of evil, when the iniquity of my heels shall compass me about? They that trust in their wealth, and boast themselves in the multitude of their riches; None of them can by any means redeem his brother, nor give to God a ransom for him: [For the redemption of their soul is precious, and it ceaseth for ever:] That he should still live for ever, and not see corruption. For he seeth that wise men die, likewise the fool and the brutish person perish, and leave their wealth to others. Their inward thought is, that their houses shall continue for ever, and their dwelling places to all generations; they call their lands after their own names. Nevertheless man being in honour abideth not: he is like the beasts that perish. This their way is folly: yet their posterity approve their sayings. Selah. Like sheep they are laid in a grave; death shall feed on them: and the upright shall have dominion over them in the morning, and their beauty shall consume in the grave from their dwelling. But God will redeem my soul from the power of the grave: for He shall forgive me. Selah. Be not thou afraid when one is made rich, when the glory of his house is increased; For when he dieth he shall carry nothing away: his glory shall not descend after him."

Where are you placing your trust? Are you trusting in your own abilities? Is your trust in your 401-K, your business, your job, your possessions, your family, your wife, your husband, your parents or your children? If your trust is in what you can see, feel, hear or anything tangible or of this earth you can become greatly disappointed; for all those things are fleeting and at any moment can let you down. Only God is unmovable and only trust in Him is marked with assurance and security.

In Psalm 56:3-4 David wrote, "what time I am afraid I will trust in thee. In God I will praise His Word, in God I have put my trust: I will not fear what flesh can do unto me." David had learned that fear of man and all that would cause fear in the natural was not even to be considered. That when ever he would begin to give in to fear he would turn and praise God for His word, His promises and fully trust in Him. David speaks to us in the same way to trust fully in God for He alone is our refuge. He put it this way in Psalm 62:7-8, "In God is my salvation and my glory; the rock of my strength, and my refuge, is in God. Trust in Him at all times ye people, pour out your heart before Him. God is a refuge for us. Selah." We need to take David's advice and pause and think about it. First of all we are not saved by our own strength or devices. Our works can't save us; our money can't save us, our devises can't save us nor can our wisdom or knowledge save us. Salvation is the free gift of God provided by the shed blood of Jesus Christ who paid the price and suffered our punishment taking our sins upon Himself. God is also our glory. We have no glory in ourselves or our accomplishments. Only what we do for Christ will last. The only strength we have , whether in the natural or in the spiritual comes from God. We are not people of our own making. If you think within yourself that you can evolve and become great through your own strength and intelligence then try to answer the questions God put to Job. Where were you when He created all? It is God alone that can protect you. Your weapons or your underground bunkers will not protect you or spare you in the day of wrath. Trust in God at all times. Abide in the Lord and let His word abide in you. Put all you are and all you desire into His hands and He is your salvation. Trust Him to be your all in all. If we are going to fear anything then fear the Lord for we are told in verse 11 of Psalm 15, that those who fear the Lord put their trust in Him and He is their help and protection.

Solomon, whom the Lord granted great wisdom and understanding writes in Proverbs 3:5, "Trust in the Lord with all thine heart; and lean not unto thine own understanding." If anyone could have been capable of trusting in his own wisdom and understanding it would have been Solomon, but because of his understanding he knew his trust must be in the Lord. The more we know the more we understand how little we know, and the more we realize the value, importance and need there is in trusting in the Lord with all of our hearts.

Isaiah shows the inner peace and joy that comes from that trust and Isaiah 12:2-3 paints that picture very well. "Behold, God is my salvation, I will trust, and not be afraid, for the Lord JEHOVAH is my strength and my song: He also is become my salvation. Therefore with joy shall ye draw water out of the wells of salvation." When we abide in the Lord understanding all He has provided in salvation, fear vanishes, we are strengthened and Christ becomes our song ringing out for all to hear. Not only shall we draw water out of the wells of salvation and never thirst for the things of this world, there shall flow rivers of living water from our most intimate being as the Spirit of God ministers to the world. What a wonderful joy and power comes from fully trusting in the Lord. We can stand and survive the rapid changes that come our way as we trust and abide in the Vine.

In Paul's writings to Timothy he both teaches and admonishes but through it all he constantly reminds Timothy to trust in the Lord in any and all circumstances. He writes this in I Timothy 4:7-10. "But refuse profane and old wives fables, and exercise thyself rather unto godliness. For bodily exercise profiteth little but godliness is profitable unto all things having promise of the life that now is of that which is to come. This is a faithful saying and worthy of all acceptation. For therefore we both labour and suffer reproach, because we trust in the living God who is the Saviour of all men, specially of those that believe."

Paul, who knew full well what it was like to face hardships, having been met with rapid change after rapid change, knew the importance of being prepared for what ever he would face. He knew the value of being physically fit but he put the greatest value and emphasis upon spiritual preparedness and because of this his emphasis was placed upon putting your trust in the living God. Today, too many people put their trust in dead idols. Now you may say to me, Chuck, 'I don't worship idols, I worship the living God!' and I would say to you that if you are trusting in yourself, your abilities, talents or anything other than God you are trusting in a dead idol. In I Timothy 6:17 Paul reminds Timothy to remind others. "Charge them that are rich in the world, that they be not highminded nor trust in uncertain riches but in the living God, who giveth us richly all things to enjoy:"

In order to make it through the rapid changes we face that come to wipe us out it is vital that we maintain our integrity and our trust in God. In order to do this our faith must never waver. Remember that faith requires faithfulness to be effective. Our faith without action is a dead faith not being actively effective and being dead does not accomplish anything. As we keep all this in mind look with me at a few scriptures on faith. First look at Romans 1:17. "For therein is the righteousness of God revealed from faith to faith: as it is written, the just shall live by faith." Remember that God gives unto every man a measure of faith. Without that faith no man could come to God for it is by faith that we are saved. Understand God's holiness and righteousness and placing us in right standing with God comes only by the faithfulness of God as He reveals to us from faith His righteousness creating faith within us to believe and the just, [those justified by faith, having been saved] shall live by faith. Faith is much more than a simple statement. Faith requires trust. Faith requires integrity. We don't get faith by sticking our heads in the sand. Romans 10:17 says, "So then faith cometh by hearing and hearing by the word of God." You may think you have strong faith but until you are tested by rapid after rapid *coming your way and rapid changes you will have little understanding of how strong your faith really is. Your faith is only as strong as your relationship in Christ and in His word. II Corinthians 1:24 says, "Not for that we have dominion over your faith, but are helpers of your joy: for by faith ye stand." Galatians 2:20 says, I am crucified with Christ, Nevertheless I live, yet not I but Christ liveth in me, and the life which I now live, I live by the faith of the Son of God, who loved me and gave himself for me." From our past discussions of this verse you should remember that it is not by our faith in the Son of God that we live but it is by the faith [OF] the Son of God that we live. It was because of His faith in knowing that only through the action of His faithfulness of going to the cross that we could receive forgiveness of sins as He bore them and that in Him we could have life. Our faith points us to Christ. His faith provides us life and by faith we stand. Strong faith requires an understanding of God's word and a uniting of our faith which is small with God's faith which is complete. When things come our way and appear to be more than we can handle or bear we need to remember to turn to all God tells us in His word. James1:2-4 reads, "My brethren count it all joy when ye fall into divers temptations; knowing that the trying of your faith worketh patience. But let patience have her perfect work that ye may be perfect and entire, wanting nothing." And I Peter 1:7 says, " That the trial of your faith being much more precious than of gold that perisheth though it be tried with fire might be found unto praise and honour and glory at the appearing of Jesus Christ."*

If our faith is weak we will falter in the times of trouble and testing but it is God's desire that in and through those times we would come unto perfection. Remember we live by the faith of the Son of God and it is only as we exercise the faith we have and understand that our faith is totally dependent upon our life in the Word, that we will be able to stand when things get rough. Our integrity and trust are based upon our faith. it is one thing to live of and walk in faith but it is another thing to be content doing it. In order to live a victorious life when rapid changes come to destroy you and take all you hold dear requires learning to be content. This is probably one of the most difficult lessons to learn if not the most difficult!

I Timothy 6:6-8 reads, "But godliness with contentment is great gain. For we brought nothing into this world and it is certain we can carry nothing out. And having food and raiment let us be therewith content." We didn't bring anything into the world with us and we can't take anything with us when we die so that being the case and the way things are we need to learn contentment instead of living a life of dissatisfaction. In Philippians 4 Paul tells us that he has learned to be content and explains how. Philippians 4:11-13 says, "Not that I speak in respect of want; for I have learned in whatsoever state I am, therewith to be content. I know both how to be abased, and I know how to abound: everywhere and in all things I am instructed both to be full and to be hungry, both to abound and to suffer need. I can do all things through Christ which strengtheneth me."

Notice that Paul says he was instructed. He was taught everywhere and in everything he faced and endured to be content. Paul learned the lessons as he faced each one because he understood that it was in Christ that he lived and moved and had his being and that if that were true, and it is, he could do all things through Christ who gave him life and strength. Contentment is only possible as you live and walk in faith in the Spirit living and abiding in Christ. Each time you successfully pass a test you learn from it and finally contentment should become a part of your life as it was with Paul. Paul not only learned to deal with riches and poverty, hunger and abundance he also learned to deal with the major life threatening direction altering events that came upon him and went contently through them in joy giving praise and glory unto God as he was victorious in contentment. Paul endured more than probably any of us will ever be called upon to face. Rapid changes do and will come crashing down upon us but just remember Christ is always with you and like Paul we too can learn to be content through every sudden change and every rapid that comes our way as we grow in the abiding life in Jesus Christ.

Chapter XIII
"A Victorious Finish"

No race is complete until the finish line is crossed. In the natural there is more than one way to finish a race. You might place 1st, 2nd, 3rd or 150th and there is always the thrill of victory and the agony of defeat. But in the race of life there are only two choices. The thrill of victory or the agony of defeat. However the thrill of victory can be marred by loss of rewards and crowns which were meant to be yours, for remember only what you do for Christ will last and we will look at this more closely as we go through the chapter.

If you have developed an intimate relationship with the Lord and have learned to walk in the Spirit content in all things, and if you are living and abiding in the vine and His word abiding in you, you can look forward to a victorious finish. But if your life is wrought with sin and you are trusting in anything other than salvation through the shed blood of Jesus Christ you have only the fearful looking forward to the judgement and the agony of defeat. What awaits you at the finish line?

In Psalm 98:1 we read, "O Sing unto the Lord a new song, for He hath done Marvelous things: His right hand and His holy arm hath gotten Him the victory." Like everything else we have faced in the river of life we need to realize that the final victory we will experience as we enter into the presence of the Lord, came about as the Lord himself gained the ultimate victory over man's enemy Satan as He defeated him on the cross. In Isaiah 25:8 we are told that He,"The Lord" shall swallow up death in victory: and the

Lord God will wipe away all tears from off our faces; and the rebuke of His people shall he take away from all the earth: for the Lord hath spoken it." What a marvelous thought to know that all the sadness and tears we have experienced in this life will be wiped away and death will have no power over those that are His.

Whether we cross the finish line facing physical death or in the rapture meet Him in the air; if we are one with Christ, and abiding in Him, we are assured of victory. I Corinthians 15:52-58 reads, "In a moment, in the twinkling of an eye, at the last trump: for the trumpet shall sound, and the dead shall be raised incorruptible, and we shall be changed. For this corruptible must put on incorruption and this mortal must put on immortality. So when this corruptible shall have put on incorruption; and this mortal shall have put on immortality, then shall be brought to pass the saying that is written, Death is swallowed up in victory. O death, where is thy sting? O grave, where is thy victory? The sting of death is sin; and the strength of sin is the law. But thanks be to God, which giveth us the victory through our Lord Jesus Christ. Therefore my beloved brethren, be ye steadfast, unmovable, always abounding in the work of the Lord, forasmuch as ye know that your labour is mot in vain in the Lord." Whether you have just begun to run the race or are nearing the finish line always remember that what you do for Christ will last and your labour is not in vain. There is great victory ahead for those who abide in the Vine. When we think of victory and the final victory of crossing the finish line we need to keep in mind that we entered the victory lap when we accepted Jesus as Lord and Saviour. I John 5:4-5 reads, "For whatsoever is born of God overcometh the world: and this is the victory that overcometh the world, even our faith. Who is he that overcometh the world, but he that believeth that Jesus is the Son of God?"

If you haven't entered the victory lap then final victory does not lie ahead but instead only the agony of defeat in outer darkness. What is the difference between those who know they are on the victory lap and those who think they are but aren"t? There are many who will face that day only to hear depart from Me ye that work iniquity. In Matthew 7:21-27 it reads, "Not everyone that saith unto Me Lord, Lord, shall enter into the kingdom of heaven; but he that doeth the will of My Father which is in heaven. Many will say to Me in that day, Lord, Lord, have we not prophesied in Thy name? and in Thy name have cast out devils? and in Thy name done many wonderful works? And then will I profess unto them, I never knew you: depart from Me , ye that work iniquity. Therefore whosoever heareth these sayings of Mine, and doeth them, I will liken him unto a wise man, which built his house upon a rock: And the rain descended, and the floods came, and the winds blew, and beat upon the house; and it fell not; for it was founded upon a rock. And everyone that heareth these sayings of mine, and doeth them not shall be likened unto a foolish man, which built his house upon the sand; and the rain descended, and the floods came and the winds blew, and beat upon that house, and it fell and great was the fall of it." You cannot live in an abiding relationship in the Vine and be unproductive. If you have paid close attention throughout our complete study and made application then you are a doer not simply a hearer of the word and you will be a fruitful branch assured of victory abiding in the love of the Lord and full of Christ's joy, knowing throughout your journey that a victorious finish awaits you and that you life has been and will continue to be effective in prayer. But if you have been doing things in your own strength and simply been a hearer of the word, not abiding in Christ or He in you or His word in you, there is no victory. Our entire study on the abiding life in Jesus Christ or 'Abide In The Vine' has been based on John 15:1-11 so let's take one last look at that portion of Scripture. Now if you have already gleaned everything there is to get out of it then what are you doing reading this book? "I am the Vine and My Father is the husbandman. Every branch in Me that beareth not fruit He taketh away: and every branch that beareth fruit, He purgeth it, that it may bring forth more fruit. Now ye are clean through the word which I have spoken unto you. Abide in Me and I in you as the branch cannot bear fruit of itself, except it abide in the vine; no more can ye except ye abide in Me. I am the Vine, ye are the branches: He that abideth in Me and I in him, the same bringeth forth much fruit; for without Me ye can do nothing. If a man abide not in me, he is cast forth as a branch, and is withered; and men gather them, and cast them into the fire, and they are burned. If ye abide in Me, and My words abide in you, ye shall ask what ye will, and it shall be done unto you. Herein is My Father glorified, that ye bear much fruit; so shall ye be My disciples. As the Father hath loved Me, so have I loved you: continue ye in My love. If ye keep My commandments, ye shall abide in My love; even as I have kept My Father's commandments, and abide in His love. These things have I spoken unto you, that My joy might remain in you and that your joy might be full."

Now I'm not going to go back to the beginning of our race in the river of life for by now we should all have a solid understanding of what it means and what is entailed in our abiding in the Vine. I pray that all who read these pages grow in a true abiding relationship in the Lord and reach a victorious finish and all that entails. I do want to remind us emphatically, and I will keep reminding us so we will never forget that being fruitful and joyful, living with answered prayers in the presence of God is the Lord's promise and His desire for each of us. As you abide in the Vine and His word abides in you, that is what will be your daily walk and the ushering in of a victorious finish. So, what awaits you as you finish the race course and enter into the victory Circle?

There are a number of things that await you: the first being what we find in the parable Jesus told of the talents which is a story of Christ's return. In Matthew 25:19-21 it reads, "After a long time the lord of those servants cometh, and reckoneth with them. And so he that had received five talents came and brought other five talents saying, Lord, thou deliverest unto me five talents: behold I have gained beside them five talents more. His lord said unto him, Well done, thou good and faithful servant: thou hast been faithful over a few things, I will make thee ruler over many things: enter thou into the joy of thy lord." As it is, in the parable, when you stand in victory before the Lord, He will say to you, "Well Done." No more wonderful words will ever you hear. The second thing that will await you upon your arrival is that you will receive a place of rulership. We will rule and reign with Christ Jesus eternally. What a fantastic thing it is to know that we will reign with Him forever and that our job never ends. The third thing that awaits you are the words you will hear your Lord say to "enter into the joy of the Lord." It was for that joy of receiving you and I into heaven that He willingly went to the cross. Christ will stand in judgement and we all shall appear before Him. II Corinthians says in chapter 5 and verse 10, "For we must all appear before the judgement seat of Christ: that every one may receive the things done in his body, according to that he hath done whether it be good or bad."

It is the desire of the Lord to meet you and reward you and I in the victory circle, not stand and judge us and pronounce, "I never knew you." Let's look at the first nine verses and ten again of II Corinthians 5. "For we know that if our earthly house of this tabernacle were dissolved, we have a building of God, and house not made with hands, eternal in the heavens. For in this we groan, earnestly desiring to be clothed upon with our house which is from heaven: If so be that being clothed we shall not be found naked. For we that are in this tabernacle do groan, being burdened: not for that we would be unclothed, but clothed upon, that mortality might be swallowed up of life. Now He that hath wrought us for the selfsame thing is God, who also hath given unto us the earnest of the Spirit. Therefore we are always confident, knowing that, whilst we are at home in the body, we are absent from the Lord: (For we walk by faith, not by sight:) We are confident, I say, and willing rather to be absent from the body, and to be present with the Lord. Wherefore we labour, that, whether present or absent, we may be accepted of Him. For we must all appear before the judgement seat of Christ; that every one may receive the things done in his body, according to that he hath done, whether it be good or bad." There is coming a day when we will have a new home and a glorified body and shall share for all eternity in the glory of the Lord when we stand before Him and He stands with us; but remember that reaching that goal and crossing the finish line in victory and entering into the rest provided and receiving the covenanted crowns requires something of us as Paul says in II Timothy 2:3-5. "Thou therefore endure hardness as a good soldier of Jesus Christ. No man that warreth entangleth himself with the affairs of this life; that he may please him who hath chosen him to be a soldier. And if a man also strive for masteries, yet is he not crowned, except he strive lawfully."

Living and abiding in Christ requires a separation from the things of this life and a total concentration upon Him, His word and living by His commandments. Like they say in the military, you follow orders as given. In Hebrews we are told that God has provided a rest for all who follow. We are also told that many for whom that rest was prepared failed to enter in because of unbelief, because of sin. Hebrews 3:12-14 reads, "Take heed, brethren, lest there be in any of you an evil heart of unbelief in departing from the living God. But exhort one another daily, while it is called to day; lest any of you be hardened through the deceitfulness of sin. For we are made partakers of Christ, if we hold the beginning of our confidence stedfast unto the end;" Then we are told in Hebrews 4:9-13, *"There remaineth therefore a rest to the people of God. For he that is entered into his rest, he also hath ceased from his own works, as God did from His. Let us labour therefore to enter into that rest, lest any man fall after the same example of unbelief. For the Word of God is quick, and powerful, and sharper that any twoedged sword, piercing even to the dividing asunder of soul and spirit and of the joints and marrow and is a discerner of the thoughts and intents of the heart. Neither is there any creature that is not manifest in His sight; but all things are naked and opened unto the eyes of Him with whom we have to do."*

No matter how close we are to crossing the finish line we must remain steadfast to the end, resisting anything that could come to cause us to stumble. Remember all is revealed to the Lord and His Word is a daily discerner of the thoughts and intents of our hearts. If you endure unto the end you will also hear the words of Christ say to you, "Enter into thy rest." Christ is the first born of the resurrection but as each of us crosses the finish line, and enter His presence, death has no hold on us, as we too receive resurrection life having already attained that when we accepted His free gift of Salvation. It will be at that point we will come to fully understand eternal life free from pain and death. There, as well as the words of "well done enter into the joy of the Lord and into thy rest" we shall receive crowns.

I Corinthians 9:25 says, "And every man that striveth for the mastery is temperate in all things. Now they do it to obtain a corruptible crown; but we an incorruptible." The crowns we receive are eternal and many. Paul tells us in II Timothy 4: 7-8 this, "I have fought a good fight I have finished my course I have kept the faith: Henceforth there is laid up for me a crown of righteousness, which the Lord, the righteous judge, shall give me at that day; and not to me only but unto all them also that love his appearing." And John writing the words of Jesus in Revelation 2:10 says, "Fear none of those things which thou shalt suffer: behold, the devil shall cast some of you into prison, that ye may be tried; and ye shall have tribulation ten days: be thou faithful unto death, and I will give thee a crown of life." We see another crown mentioned in I Peter 5:4. "And when the Chief Shepherd shall appear, ye shall receive a crown of glory that fadeth not away." James 1:12 says, "Blessed is the man that endureth temptation: for when he is tried, he shall receive the crown of life, which the Lord hath promised to them that love Him."

Awaiting you are crowns and blessings, words of praise and achievement awards but also new names and even a secret name between only you and the Lord. Revelation 2:17 says, "He that hath an ear, let him hear what the Spirit saith unto the churches; To him that overcometh will I give to eat of the hidden manna and I will give him a white stone, and in the stone a new name written, which no man knoweth saving he that receiveth it." The relationship you develop with the Lord here on earth is to be an intimate abiding relationship and He deals with every relationship in a personal way. Not only does He give you a new name only known between you and the Lord Himself, He also puts God's name upon you and writes His new name upon you. Revelation 3:11-12 says, "Behold I come quickly: hold fast which thou hast that no man take thy crown. Him that overcometh will I make a pillar in the temple of My God and he shall go no more out: and I will write upon him the name of My God, and the name of the city of My God which is New Jerusalem, which cometh down out of heaven from my God: And I will write upon him My new name."

The Lord also says we will be clothed in white and He will confess us before the Father. So what is required of us to enter the victory circle? **Separation from the world,** *faithfulness, endurance, commitment and an intimate abiding relationship in Christ and the word. But first and most important is a surrendered life to Jesus Christ and belief in what He did and acceptance of God's free gift of salvation through the shed blood of Jesus Christ. He gives us the ability and means to be separated from the world, become faithful and endure as we abide in Him.*

The "Vine", the source of all life will always be; so stay attached, continue to abide and you will always be victorious and assured of the blessings of the victory circle.

Chapter IVX
"Beyond The Finish Line"

Our study on Abiding Life would not be complete without a chapter on heaven. Receiving crowns and a new name and the wonderful accolades of the victory circle would soon loose their luster if it weren't for Heaven itself and all it entails.

Since God is a creative God He would deny Himself and His own creativity if He ever ceased to create. Jesus said of the Father that, "........... My Father worketh hitherto, and I work." The Jews had sought to kill Jesus because He was performing miracles on the Sabbath but His answer to them was that God the Father was still at work. The word tells that in I Corinthians 2:9, ".......eye hath not seen nor ear heard, neither have entered into the heart of man the things which God hath prepared for them that love Him." I have a pretty vivid imagination and I could write volumes on what I can imagine in my heart that God has in store for us in heaven and yet here we are told I don't even come close. Since God is a God of love, a creative God who created us in His likeness and image and who says we shall rule and reign with Him for ever, I am sure that whatever we will rule over and whatever and wherever in the vast universe, first created for light for man here upon this small planet, that we shall each reign shall be magnificent and created to meet each and every personality that shall be received into heaven with our Lord. But then it isn't my description that counts. So let's look back at what "The Word' says to us.

There are a number of things that endure and last forever. God is eternal. God the Father, God the Son and God the Holy Spirit will never cease. The Word of God is eternal.

Heaven and Earth as we know them now will pass away but God's word will never pass away. Faith will go on forever, love will never cease and hope will spring eternal. God's mercy is everlasting. Psalm 9:7 says, "But the Lord shall endure forever. He hath prepared His throne for judgement." If anyone thinks he will escape judgement, God, says no, it isn't going to happen. The Lord endures forever and judgement will happen. Psalm 104:31 says, "The glory of the Lord shall endure for ever: the Lord shall rejoice in His works." The 136th Psalm says over and over, as it speaks of all the wonderful things the Lord has done, that His mercy endures forever. As you and I enter into eternity we will come to understand the wonders of God that are eternal and lasting, what His mercy has provided and the presence of His glory. In the book of Isaiah chapter 57 and verse 15 we see that God, who is eternal in the heavens is there to receive all who enter in and we too will share eternity forever. "For thus saith the High and Lofty One that inhabiteth eternity, whose name is Holy; I dwell in the high and holy place, with Him also that is of a contrite and humble spirit, to revive the spirit of the humble and to revive the heart of the contrite ones."

I realize it is hard to envision stepping from mortality to immortality and going from humanity to eternity but it shall happen in the twinkling of an eye. We know that salvation and eternal life only come through acceptance of the free gift of Christ's atoning blood so how do we handle the portion of scripture in Matthew 25:31-46 which appears to say eternity is based on works. "When the Son of man shall come in His glory, and all the holy angels with Him, then shall He sit upon the throne of His glory: And before Him shall be gathered all nations: and He shall separate them one from another, as a shepherd divideth his sheep from the goats: And He shall set the sheep on His right hand, but the goats on the left. Then shall the King say unto them on His right hand, Come, ye blessed of My Father. Inherit the kingdom prepared for you from the foundation of the world: For I was an hungred, and ye gave me meat: I was thirsty and you gave Me drink; I was a stranger and ye took Me in: Naked and ye clothed Me: I was sick, and ye visited Me: I was in prison and ye came unto Me: Then shall the righteous answer Him, saying Lord, when saw we Thee an hungred and fed Thee? or thirsty, and gave Thee drink? When saw we Thee a stranger, and took Thee in? or naked, and clothed Thee? Or when saw we Thee sick, or in prison and came unto thee? And the King shall answer and say unto them, Verily I say unto you, Inasmuch as ye have done it unto one of the least of these my brethren, Ye have done it unto Me. Then shall He say also unto them on the left hand, Depart from Me, ye cursed, into everlasting fire, prepared for the devil and his angels: for I was an hungred,and ye gave Me no meat: I was thirsty, and ye gave Me no drink: I was a stranger, and ye took me not in: naked, and ye clothed Me not: sick, and in prison, and ye visited Me not. Then shall they also answer Him, saying, Lord, when saw we Thee an hungred, or a thirst, or a stranger, or naked, or sick, and in prison, and did not minister unto Thee? Then shall He answer them, saying. Verily I say unto you, inasmuch as ye did it not unto one of the least of these ye did it not to Me. And these shall go away into everlasting punishment: but the righteous into life eternal." Where on the surface it does appear that works play into who goes where but the truth is in this. The Key is that those who truly love the Lord put that love into action and they don't even realize that they are doing anything out of the norm. It is an automatic reaction to living every day through Christ. On the other hand those who don't have new life in Christ never think of serving others or if they do it is for selfish reasons like the Pharisees who gave to be seen.

Salvation and your heavenly home is only determined by a single action and the mercy of God. John 3:15-18 says, "That whosoever believeth in Him should not perish, but have eternal life. For God so loved the world, that He gave

His only begotten Son that whosoever believeth in Him should not perish, but have everlasting life. For God sent not His Son into the world to condemn the world; but that the world through Him might be saved. He that believeth on Him is not condemned: but he that believeth not is condemned already, because he hath not believed in the name of the only begotten Son of God."

Make sure you know where you will spend eternity. John 6:54 makes it oh so clear that it is a total identifying of your life in Christ where you partake of His life that assures you of eternal life. "Whoso eateth My flesh, and drinketh My blood, hath eternal life; and I will raise him up at the last day." John 10:27-29 says, "My sheep hear My voice, and I know them, and they follow Me: And I give unto them eternal life, and they shall never perish, neither shall and man pluck them out of My hand. My Father, which gave them Me, is greater than all; and no man is able to pluck them out of My Father's hand." Jesus says that if we are His we know His voice and follow Him. We are not simple hearers but doers of the word and He gives us eternal life which no one can take away. When we think of the eternal we are constantly reminded that there is much which now is hidden and invisible to us. Now we see as through a glass darkly but then face to face. II Corinthians 4:17-18 reads, "For our light affliction, which is but for a moment, worketh for us a far more exceeding and eternal weight of glory: While we look not at the things which are seen, but at the things which are not seen: for the things which are seen are temporal: but the things which are not seen are eternal." We can look forward to many blessings which are now invisible.

If we suffer with Christ we know that as heirs and joint heirs we will rule and reign with Christ Jesus throughout eternity which is a wonderful thought. But if you are abiding in the Lord and have received the abundance of grace and the gift of righteousness, you shall reign, in life, by Jesus Christ and that reign extends to eternal life. Romans 5:17 and 21 reads, "For if by one man's offense death reigned by one; much more they which receive abundance of grace and the gift of righteousness shall reign in life by one, Jesus Christ.) .... That as sin hath reigned unto death, even so might grace reign through righteousness unto eternal life by Jesus Christ our Lord." Just as eternal life begins the moment you accept God's free gift through Christ you reign with Him from that moment on, although how we reign here is far different than the reign we will experience in heaven.

If you wish to reign with the Lord then you must identify with the Lord. II Timothy 2:12, "If we suffer, we shall also reign with Him: it we deny Him, He also will deny us:" Revelation 11:15 tells us that Christ shall reign for ever and remember we shall reign with Him, "And the seventh angel sounded; and there were great voices in heaven, saying, The kingdoms of this world are become the kingdoms of our Lord and of His Christ: and He shall reign forever and ever." Revelation 20:6 says, "Blessed and holy is he that hath part in the first resurrection: on such the second death hath no power, but they shall be priests of God and of Christ, and shall reign with Him a thousand years." And Revelation 22:5 says, "And there shall be no night there; and they need no candle neither light of the sun, for the Lord God giveth them light, and they shall reign for ever and ever." Since God is light which enlightens every soul, where He is there can be no darkness, so as we reign we need never be concerned with darkness.

Another aspect of heaven is the lack of tears, sorrow, pain and death. Revelation 21:4 reads, "And God shall wipe away all tears from their eyes; and there shall be no more death, neither sorrow, nor crying, neither shall there be any more pain: for the former things are passed away." That which was once in the garden of Eden shall appear in our heavenly home. The tree of life will be with us eternally.

Revelation 2:7 reads, "He that hath an ear, let him hear what the Spirit saith unto the churches; To him that overcometh will I give to eat of the tree of life, which is in the midst of the paradise of God." Revelation 22:2 reads, "In the midst of the street of it, and on either side of the river was there the tree of life, which bare twelve manner of fruits, and yielded her fruit every month: and the leaves of the tree were for the healing of the nations." And 22:14 says, "Blessed are they that do His commandments, that they may have right to the tree of life and may enter in through the gate into the city." It was disobedience that kept Adam and Eve from the blessings of the tree of life and it is obedience that will make a way for us.

All the thrills and all the blessings that await us in eternity in God's presence are specially and individually for each and every one who has chosen to accept all the Lord has done for them and chosen to abide in Him and have His word abide in them, having left the things of the world to live and walk in the Spirit of God seeking Christ in all His fulness daily and serving Him and looking for His blessed return. Those who have and those who are keeping the commandments of the Lord are assured by Jesus' own words that He has gone to prepare a place for each of them. Is that you? John 14:1-3 reads, "Let not your heart be troubled: ye believe in God, believe also in Me. In My Father's house are many mansions: if it were not so, I would have told you. I go to prepare a place for you. And if I go and prepare a place for you, I will come again, and receive you unto Myself; that where I am, there ye may be also." Jesus relationship with each and every believer is personal and you can be certain that His preparations will far exceed anything you see on extreme makeover.

If you look closely at all that is written in both old and new testaments you will find a description of the heavenly kingdom, the New Jerusalem and the temple of our God that will completely hypnotize you with the extreme beauty.

I'm not going to rewrite all the prophetic scriptures here. I will let you feed upon the word and do that when you have time. I am simply going to touch here on a very few descriptive passages from Revelation and Hebrews. Hebrews 11:10 says, "For he looked for a city which hath foundations, whose builder and maker is God." We should all be like Abraham just passing through this life looking forward for all God has prepared for us. The spiritual foundation for that city is built upon Jesus Christ and His word. Each and everyone who names the name of Christ is also part of that master building but the actual physical structure of the new Jerusalem and our heavenly kingdom is being and has been built by God and what a place it is. Revelation 21:10-14 and 18-23 describes it this way. "And he carried me away in the spirit to a great and high mountain, and showed me that great city, the holy Jerusalem, descending out of heaven form God, Having the glory of God: and her light was like unto a stone most precious, even like a jasper stone, clear as crystal: and had a wall great and high, and had twelve gates and at the gates twelve angels, and the names written thereon, which are the names of the twelve tribes of the children of Israel: On the east three gates; on the north three gates; on the south three gates ; and on the west three gates. And the wall of the city had twelve foundations, and in them the names of the twelve apostles of the Lamb. .... and the building of the wall of it was of jasper: and the city was of pure gold, like unto clear glass. And the foundations of the wall of the city were garnished with all manner of precious stones. The first foundation was jasper; the second, sapphire; the third, a chalcedony; the fourth, an emerald; the fifth, sardonyx; the sixth, sardius, the seventh, chrysolyte; the eighth, beryl; the ninth, a topaz; the tenth, a chrysoprasus, the eleventh, a jacinth; the twelfth, an amethyst. And the twelve gates were twelve pearls; every several gate was of one pearl: and the street of the city was of pure gold, as it were transparent glass. And I saw no temple therein; for the Lord God almighty and the Lamb are the temple of it, and the city had no need of sun, neither of the moon, to shine in it: for the glory of God did lighten it and the Lamb is the light thereof." Wow! Something tells me you better have your sunglasses. Well, not really. But, such glory is hard to even begin to fathom.

Let us remember that beyond the finish line is a whole new world, with a new heaven and new earth, new experiences and great joys. But also remember that the blessings of heaven are dependent upon our intimate abiding relationship in the Vine here and now as we are on the earth walking and living in the Spirit, keeping the Lord's commandments while looking for His return and all the time being vigilant to love and serve God with all your heart and soul and mind and strength and with God's eternal love daily serving man.

Proverbs 27:27 reads, "As in water face answereth to face, so the heart of man to man." The reflection we should see in the river of life looking back at us is the reflection of Jesus Christ as we abide in Him living at face level in the river of life and are daily being made into His likeness and His Image. May your journey be a safe one filled with the love and joy of the Lord and may you experience the thrill of victory!

Chuck Lamka has been involved in ministry for 42 years and has served the Lord in many lands as a pastor, Bible teacher, radio minister and missionary evangelist and since 1977 as the founding director of Little Light Ministries Unlimited and can be reached at 10611 Canyon Rd E PMB 230 Puyallup WA. USA or charleslamka@gmail.com

www.ingramcontent.com/pod-product-compliance
Lightning Source LLC
Chambersburg PA
CBHW060750050426
42449CB00008B/1339